PRESENTING

M. E. Kerr

Twayne's United States Authors Series
Young Adult Authors

Patricia J. Campbell, General Editor

TUSAS 678

Reading and writing have always gone together for M. E. Kerr, shown here in her home library.

PRESENTING

M. E. Kerr

Updated Edition

Alleen Pace Nilsen

Twayne Publishers
An Imprint of Simon & Schuster Macmillan
New York

Prentice Hall International
London Mexico City New Delhi Singapore Sydney Toronto

Twayne's United States Authors Series No. 678

Presenting M.E. Kerr, Updated Edition
Alleen Pace Nilsen

Twayne Publishers
An Imprint of Simon & Schuster Macmillan
1633 Broadway
New York, NY 10019–6785

Library of Congress Cataloging-in-Publication Data

Nilsen, Alleen Pace.
    Presenting M. E. Kerr / Alleen Pace Nilsen. — Updated ed.
        p.   cm. — (Twayne's United States authors series ; TUSAS 678. Young adult authors)
    Includes bibliographical references and index.
    Summary: A critical introduction to the life and work of the young adult novelist M. E. Kerr.
    ISBN 0–8057–9248–1 (alk. paper)
    1. Kerr, M. E.—Criticism and interpretation.   2. Women and literature—United States—History—20th century.   3. Young adult fiction, American—History and criticism.   [1. Kerr, M. E.—Criticism and interpretation.   2. American literature—History and criticism.]   I. Title.   II. Series: Twayne's United States authors series ; TUSAS 678.   III. Series: Twayne's United States authors series. Young adult authors.
    PS3561.E643Z786 1997
    813′.54—dc21   96–39134
                                                                                            CIP
                                                                                            AC

The paper used in this publication meets the minimum requirements of American National Standard for Information Services—Permanence of Paper for Printed Library Materials. ANSI Z39.48-1984. ∞™

10 9 8 7 6 5 4 3 2 1

Printed in the United States of America

To
Don L. F. Nilsen
still my good humor man

Contents

Preface

As I said in the 1986 edition of this book, anyone listing today's best writers for young adults would have to place M. E. Kerr very near the top. Both her writing ability and her consistency in producing so many highly acclaimed and popular books prompt me to make this claim. In 1993 I was pleased to have this statement substantiated when the Young Adult Library Services Association of the American Library Association chose Kerr as the fifth winner of the Margaret A. Edwards award. The association accords this honor to an author whose books "have provided young adults with a window through which they can view the world, and which will help them to grow and understand themselves and their role in society."

Returning after a decade to rewrite *Presenting M. E. Kerr* reminded me of attending a tenth-year high school reunion and being happily surprised at how much a favorite classmate had accomplished; in addition, the whole class seemed much smarter. Not only did I have twice as many Kerr novels to read and enjoy but I also found more thoughtful articles and reviews as well as autobiographical statements by Kerr. I still hope that reading this volume will not take the place of delving into M. E. Kerr's books; rather, I trust that this new edition will encourage adults as well as teenagers to read her stories with more insight and pleasure.

Two major changes—one technological and one social—make this a better book than the first edition, which was written with the help of notecards, yellow pads, and a typewriter. A word processor has made it easier for me to rethink observations and to draw together and analyze certain pervasive characteristics of

Kerr's writing. These include her cleverness in creating names, her skill with dialogue, her contagious enthusiasm for intriguing facts, and her ability to leave readers with topics to ponder after their smiles have faded. Moreover, social changes of the early 1990s have had a positive impact on this revision. At that time, cultural attitudes had evolved to the point that Kerr felt comfortable in publicly acknowledging the lesbian identity that had always played a role in her developing empathy for the underdog (see chapter 8) and her understanding of the frustration that nearly all teenagers feel as they straddle two worlds: the childhood they are leaving and the adulthood they are trying to enter.

I am grateful to M. E. Kerr, whose real name is Marijane Meaker, for being generous with her time and thoughts when I interviewed her on 28 May 1985 and again on 9 January 1996. Statements from her that are quoted or paraphrased throughout this book and not attributed to other sources come from these interviews. I am also grateful to Ron Brown for inviting me to embark on the first edition of *Presenting M. E. Kerr* and to Patty Campbell for giving me a second chance. William Morris at HarperCollins and John Mason at Scholastic deserve thanks for sending review copies and other information. My husband, Don Nilsen, helped me perceive Kerr's skill at using humor and word play for more than simply amusing her readers. Among the friends and colleagues who helped are Ken Donelson, who pulled from his bookshelves a copy of *The Well of Loneliness* that Kerr talks about in chapter 8, and Dawn Bates, who helped me make fewer errors than I might have in relation to complicated issues surrounding homosexuality. Finally, I want to thank my students at Arizona State University who over the years have provided stimulation and thought as they have read and responded to Kerr's books.

Chronology

1927 Marijane Meaker born 27 May in Auburn, New York.

1943 Leaves Auburn to attend Stuart Hall school in Staunton, Virginia.

1945 Is suspended from Stuart Hall in February but allowed to return in April and graduate with her class. Attends Vermont Junior College, where she edits the school newspaper.

1946 Enrolls at the University of Missouri.

1949 Graduates from the University of Missouri as an English literature major; moves to New York to find a job in publishing.

1951 Sells "Devotedly, Patrick Henry Casebolt" (under pen name Laura Winston) to *Ladies' Home Journal*.

1952 *Spring Fire* followed over next 17 years by 17 other mysteries (under pen name Vin Packer).

1955 *We Walk Alone* followed over next few years by four other books about lesbian relationships (under pen name Ann Aldrich).

1964 *Sudden Endings* followed over next few years by three other books (under name M. J. Meaker) including *Shockproof Sydney Skate*.

1972   *Dinky Hocker Shoots Smack!* (under pen name M. E. Kerr).

1973   *If I Love You, Am I Trapped Forever?* (under pen name M. E. Kerr).

1974   *The Son of Someone Famous* (under pen name M. E. Kerr).

1975   *Is That You, Miss Blue?* and *Love Is a Missing Person* (under pen name M. E. Kerr).

1977   *I'll Love You When You're More Like Me* (under pen name M. E. Kerr).

1978   *Gentlehands* (under pen name M. E. Kerr).

1981   *Little Little* (under pen name M. E. Kerr).

1982   *What I Really Think of You* (under pen name M. E. Kerr).

1983   *ME ME ME ME ME: Not a Novel* (under pen name M. E. Kerr).

1984   *Him She Loves?* (under pen name M. E. Kerr).

1985   *I Stay Near You* (under pen name M. E. Kerr).

1986   *Night Kites* (under pen name M. E. Kerr).

1987   *Fell* (under pen name M. E. Kerr).

1989   *Fell Back* (under pen name M. E. Kerr).

1990   *Shoebag* (under pen name Mary James).

1991   *Fell Down* (under pen name M. E. Kerr).

1993   *Linger* (under pen name M. E. Kerr).

1993   Wins Margaret A. Edwards Award, presented each year by the American Library Association and *School Library Journal* to an author whose books "have provided young adults with a window through which they can view the world."

1993 *The Shuteyes* (under pen name Mary James).

1994 *Deliver Us from Evie* (under pen name M. E. Kerr).

Frankenlouse (under pen name Mary James).

1996 *Shoebag Returns* (under pen name Mary James).

1997 in press *"Hello," I Lied* (under pen name M. E. Kerr).

forthcoming *Blood on the Forehead* (under pen name M. E. Kerr).

1. The Aspiring Writer

> I wished I was Eric Ranthram McKay, back upstairs where I
> belonged, writing about life instead of enduring it.
>
> from *ME ME ME ME ME: Not a Novel*

Although M. E. Kerr was born in 1972 as a pen name on the cover
of *Dinky Hocker Shoots Smack!*, Marijane Meaker was born in
Auburn, New York, in 1927. The best place to get acquainted with
both the young Marijane and her metamorphosis, M. E. Kerr, is
in her 1983 autobiographical *ME ME ME ME ME: Not a Novel.*[1]
Marijane was the middle child and only daughter of Ida T. and
Ellis R. Meaker. Her grandfather owned the grocery stores in
town, and her father owned a factory, so she grew up feeling privileged, at least until midway through high school when she was
packed off to boarding school and was surprised to meet girls
whose fathers were CEOs' of international corporations.

In an autobiographical piece that Kerr wrote for Gale Research
Company,[2] she gave her father credit for making her into a reader
and her mother credit for making her into a people watcher and
consequently a writer. Ellis Meaker was bookish, reading everything from the Harvard classics to all the Book-of-the-Month-
Club selections and in between Dickens, Emerson, Poe, Steinbeck, and such magazines as *Time*, *Life*, *Look*, and *Fortune*. The
family living room was four walls of books, and Mr. Meaker was
constantly investigating some person or some period of history.
Marijane spent hours browsing in the town library while waiting
for her father to do his research. He kept a daily journal and
encouraged Marijane to keep a diary, explaining that "Men keep

journals, and women keep diaries." Her father was more faithful with his journal than Marijane was with her diary, and the grown-up Kerr relied on his writings for many of the memories in *ME ME ME ME ME*.

Kerr's mother was a vivacious woman filled with curiosity, and Kerr says that long before J. D. Salinger had one of his characters peek into someone else's bathroom cabinet to examine the prescription medicine being used in the household, Mrs. Meaker made this a regular part of her visiting ritual. On Saturday evenings she would take out her Chevrolet coupe, and she and Marijane would drive downtown and park at key vantage points. Mrs. Meaker would knit while keeping up a continuous stream of observations about who was going to the Auburn Palace theater with whom, which men were spending Saturday night at Boysen's Bar, and then on the way home whose house still needed painting, who was eating dinner in their dining room instead of their kitchen, and whose car was parked in whose driveway. In *The Son of Someone Famous*, this scene is played out almost word-for-word with Brenda Belle Blossom and her mother.

When Ida Meaker telephoned her friends, she would tell Marijane to go outside and play. Marijane would pretend to obey and would slam the back door on her way to hiding in the hall. Kerr maintains that eavesdropping on these phone conversations taught her how fiction spins grandly from fact. Every conversation started with "Wait 'til you hear this!" Today when Kerr considers story ideas, she asks herself if the topic could be one of her mother's wait-'til-you-hear-this telephone calls. If the answer is no, then she passes up that idea for a better one.

When Marijane was in high school, she was enchanted with the writing style of Max Shulman, author of the television comedy series *Dobie Gillis*, but her English teacher confidently predicted she would outgrow this admiration, which she did. Later on, her favorite author was Carson McCullers. When in college, Kerr read and reread *Member of the Wedding*, recognizing some of her old self in Frankie, the 12-year-old who gave herself a crewcut, changed her name to F. Jasmine Addams, and tried to go along with her brother and his bride on their honeymoon. In *ME ME*

ME ME ME, Kerr wrote "But more than I could see a 'yesterday me' in Frankie, I could see a future me in Carson McCullers. She became the one I most wanted to write like, and all my stories began to describe 'a green and crazy summer,' or 'a green queer dream' or 'a crazy queer green time,' on and on" (*ME*, 156).

ME ME ME ME ME is not the only book in which M. E. Kerr—the person—appears; it is just the most obvious. In reality, her personality is the driving force behind many of her most interesting characters. In an afterword, Kerr acknowledges the swirling together in her own mind of her autobiographical and fictional stories: "Like all true experiences that are later translated into fiction, some of it was that way, some of it wasn't that way, and sometimes the author no longer remembers what was said and what wasn't" (*ME*, 112).

Because the stories are so much fun, however, few readers are going to quibble about factual details. They are presented in approximate chronological order, spanning the period from her World War II childhood to the beginning of her career as a freelance writer.

" 'Murder' He Says" was probably chosen as the opening story because it is the most romantic and was therefore judged the most likely to interest teenage readers. It is the story of 15-year-old Marijane's "romance" with Donald Dare, the son of the local undertaker. (He later served as the prototype for the fictional Wally Witherspoon in *I'll Love You When You're More Like Me*.) Marijane and Donald's relationship, however, isn't nearly as interesting as the one between her best friend, Ella Gwen Logan, and Hyman Ginzburg. Marijane, Hyman, and Ella Gwen are the town's three library habitués. One ordinary winter afternoon when Marijane has just discovered Thomas Wolfe and is rushing to find Ella Gwen and show her a sexy passage about "black, bitter, aching loneliness," she sees Hyman and Ella Gwen kissing, right there in the stacks between Louisa May Alcott and James Joyce. This long kiss was the beginning of a "love affair that Shakespeare, MGM, or Cole Porter couldn't have made more passionate and doomed" (*ME*, 18).

When Hyman is drafted and instructed to report to Fort Knox, Kentucky, Marijane helps Ella Gwen run away with him. After this momentous event—which Marijane later characterized as "her finest hour"—the Meakers decide it is time for Marijane to go away to boarding school. They pore over the advertisements in the back pages of *Good Housekeeping* magazine and select Stuart Hall near Staunton, Virginia. Few parents ever received such an investment return, for Marijane's experiences at Stuart Hall provided her with material for a lifetime of writing. Various kinds of boarding schools play a major role in *Is That You, Miss Blue?*, *ME ME ME ME ME*, *Frankenlouse*, *Shoebag Returns*, and the three *Fell* books, and references to students traveling to and from private schools crop up in several other works.

Before Kerr shares her school experience with readers in *ME ME ME ME ME*, she presents three stories from her childhood. Before World War II, Marijane's father was a mayonnaise manufacturer. During the war, however, mayonnaise isn't considered an essential commodity, so Mr. Meaker switches over to dehydrated onions. The whole town smells like onions, and it is little comfort to Marijane that her father places apologetic ads in the local newspaper:

> Ivanhoe Foods Has Gone to War!
> Our onions are for field rations for our fighting men.
> When you smell onions, pray for peace. (*ME*, 10)

Marijane's father provides her with alternate moments of pride and chagrin. In World War I, he served in the French army, and he nostalgically wears a French beret when riding his bicycle back and forth to work. Slightly deaf, he uses a hearing aid in one ear. Every Sunday morning in church he ceremoniously takes it out and puts it away as the minister begins his sermon. He is just as obvious in replacing it before the choir begins singing.

The second story in *ME ME ME ME ME* is "Where Are You Now, William Shakespeare?" Of this period in Kerr's life, Ellis Meaker writes "Marijane is ten. She plays with boys and looks like one" (*ME*, 35). Marijane is ahead of her time in dressing in her brother's outgrown pants and old shirts, set off by one of her father's business suit vests, a cap, and Indian moccasins. She has a 10-year-old boyfriend named William Shakespeare, called Billy for short. Unlike Donald Dare, Kerr writes, he does not "call at seven for dates, or suffer my father's inspection, or give me a silver identification bracelet" (*ME,* 35). They do not have a song, either. Mostly they catch sunfish and polliwogs at Hoopes Park and talk about the future. Billy Shakespeare accepts the fact that Marijane's real hero is her father.

Marijane is sure that, if only her father were president, the country wouldn't be so beset by troubles. Although Billy not so tactfully points out that Mr. Meaker would have to be elected first, Marijane is convinced that this would present no problem. After consulting her father, she explains to Billy that the only thing standing in the way is Mr. Meaker's desire for privacy for himself and his family.

The third story is "Marijane the Spy," which is discussed in chapter 8. The fourth tale is strangely entitled "1, 2, 3, 4, 5, 6, 7, 8, 9, 10, 11, 12, 100." An explanation for the title comes early in the story: "Twelve was the age I was when my baby brother was born, and my older brother went off to military school. Thirteen was the year I became a hundred" and felt like a "nothing, sandwiched between two stars" (*ME,* 60). To boost her out of her slump, Mrs. Meaker enrolls Marijane in Laura Bryan's school for ballroom dancing. Here Marijane is trapped in a Catch-22 situation. Eager for Marijane to become a social success, Mrs. Meaker keeps wondering aloud why no boy invites Marijane to stay afterward and go to Miss Margaret's ice cream parlor for a soda. At least Clinton Klock, a boy still in his formative years and not yet "up to snuff," dances with Marijane every week between four and five, but he never mentions a soda. Finally, after weeks of Mrs. Meaker's inquisitions and Marijane's weak excuses, Marijane takes matters into her own hands and asks Clinton why they never go for a soda. When he discloses that he is saving his money to buy a boat, Marijane offers to go dutch. When he is still hesitant, Marijane offers to treat.

Having slipped Clinton the money, Marijane thinks she is going to be saved from "life's biggest embarrassment" by the fact that no one will know she is treating. During this grand social experience,

This family portrait shows Marijane before the birth of her younger brother when she suddenly felt like "a nothing, sandwiched between two stars."

Marijane unfairly signals to her friends that she knows this boy is a loser and that she has come with him only for laughs. Afterward, Clinton and Marijane find Mrs. Klock waiting in the car to give them a ride. Marijane thinks little of this until she arrives home and is met by her indignant and embarrassed mother: "Whatever got into you to tell Clinton you'd buy him a soda! When he called his mother to tell her why he'd be late getting home, she felt so ashamed, she got dressed and got out the car, to give you a ride home! She said Clinton has money of his own but he's saving for a boat, and she felt just awful!" (*ME,* 69).

Perhaps so, but Marijane feels even worse, especially when her mother goes on to preach that obviously Marijane has money to squander, and if she feels so rich why doesn't she think of buying a present for her baby brother?

"There's Not a Man in This Damn Nunnery" recounts Marijane's experiences at Stuart Hall. The first semester, her assigned roommate is Kay Walters, the first "P. K." (preacher's kid) Marijane gets to know. The next semester, she is moved next door to bunk with Agnes Thatcher, the first deaf person she becomes acquainted with.

"Your Daddy Was a Sailor" gets its title from one of the sad, romantic stories that Kerr began writing and submitting to magazines between her junior and senior years in high school. She is especially fond of this title because an editor wrote "Touching" on a rejection slip, which Marijane carried around for weeks in the back pocket of her jeans.

In 1944, the town of Auburn is full of sailors from Sampson Naval Base, which situation inspires the Meakers to buy a cottage at the most distant point on Owasco Lake and leave town during the summers. While living in the relatively isolated cottage, Marijane becomes Eric Ranthram McKay.

> By day I swam and sailed and looked after my kid brother, listening to my girl friends' accounts of what was happening, for hours on the telephone. By night I wrote, using my first pseudonym . . . chosen because my father's initials were E. R. M. After I wrote a story, I mailed it off to a magazine with a letter written on my father's stationery, engraved with his initials and our home address. (*ME,* 114)

A highlight of the summer is a visit from Jan Fox, supposedly the most sophisticated girl at Stuart Hall. Marijane, who no longer believes that her father would be president of the United States except for valuing the family's privacy, is humiliated when her father makes their dates come in and show their drivers' licenses. In a revealing line, Marijane laments "I wished I was Eric Ranthram McKay, back upstairs where I belonged, writing about life instead of enduring it" (*ME,* 122).

Kerr explains that she was probably drawn to a pen name not only because of her father's monogrammed stationery but also because she liked the idea of creating a separate identity for herself

Marijane in 1944 with Eddie, a sailor from Sampson Naval Base. She says the base and its sailors were the bane of her parents' existence. In the background is her first car, a 1937 La Salle convertible with a rumble seat.

and writing about people she knew without their ever realizing who was telling their secrets.

Although none of the stories Marijane wrote during high school—and only a few she wrote during college—were accepted for publication, her continuous recording of actions and emotions may have implanted these experiences in her mind. Unlike most adults who have forgotten—or repressed—the insecurities and the emotional highs and lows of their teen years, she can thus keep going back to the well and coming up with fresh ways to relate the hilarity and the agonies of youth.

"What I Did between Trains" describes Marijane's expulsion—or suspension (there is some disagreement about the matter)—from Stuart Hall. On her way back to school after Christmas vacation, she buys a dart board and decorates it with yearbook pictures of faculty members accompanied by disrespectful names. When this popular dormitory game is found in Marijane's closet by the house mother—and on George "Couldn't-Tell-A-Lie" Washington's birthday, no less—she is sent home.

From the end of February through March, Marijane works in a local defense plant while her mother and father write letters to get her reinstated at school. In April, she is back, but because the school yearbook was put together while she was gone, the yearbook editors could include her only at the end of the alphabet, ". . . Wellford, Worthy, and Yates . . . then Marijane Meaker, on record forever, the out-of-line black sheep" (*ME,* 144).

"The Sister of Someone Famous" recounts Marijane's first college experience. She had wanted to go to the University of Missouri School of Journalism because it was considered the best in the country. Her father argues in favor of Syracuse University in the hope that she will marry a New York boy and the Meakers can know their grandchildren. The disagreement over the choice of a college becomes a moot question when Marijane is rejected by both universities due to her poor records and recommendations from Stuart Hall. However, Vermont Junior College decides to take a chance on her. There, a wise teacher chooses her as the founding editor of a school newspaper. Her first published story is in this paper—never mind that she is the editor and practically the whole staff. A story within this story, which was the inspiration for Kerr's later book *The Son of Someone Famous,* is about one of the students whose sister is a famous movie star.

When Marijane does surprisingly well at the junior college her first year, she is accepted at the University of Missouri School of Journalism for the fall of 1946. However, she hadn't anticipated one problem: In this era of postwar growth and housing short-ages, there are no dormitories in which out-of-state students can live. If she is unable to join a sorority—so that she can live in the sorority house—she will have to return home. Her father does lit-tle to boost her confidence when he refuses to ship her trunk until after the horrendous "rush week." Even though Marijane hates much of what occurs that week, she is relieved to be invited to join Alpha Delta Pi. Kerr created the title of her sixth book, *I'll Love You When You're More Like Me,* from this experience.

Marijane is not a typical sorority sister. She feels drawn to other journalism students, most of whom are not sorority mem-bers, and to campus intellectuals as much as she does to her housemates. The journalism students encourage each other in their writing by saying that "You'll never commit suicide as long as you have a manuscript in the mail" (*ME,* 183). The trick is to keep your stories circulating. Marijane gets a literary crush on F. Scott Fitzgerald and wears out a copy of his autobiographical pieces called *The Crack-Up.* She circles words like *insouciance* and memorizes his line about good writing being like swimming underwater and holding your breath. At a sorority masquerade party, she goes as a rejection slip, wearing a full-length black slip with rejections from magazines pinned to it.

During the summer of 1948, Marijane falls in love with a Hun-garian refugee who is a revolutionary of sorts, joins the Commu-nist party, and starts working as a volunteer at the Fulton mental hospital. When her radical young man grows too busy for her and does things that disillusion her, she begins dating the head psy-chiatrist at the mental hospital. She also dates an English major and switches her program from journalism to English literature after deciding she does not want to be restricted to facts. She wants the freedom of adding her own ideas and conjectures. Else-where she confesses that the decision to change was also influ-enced by the fact that she failed economics, which was a basic requirement for journalism majors.

The concluding chapter of *ME ME ME ME ME* is entitled "New York" and describes how, after graduation, Marijane moves with two other Missouri graduates to New York City, where she manages to get hired and fired by nine different companies in a single year. Then, on April 20, 1951, when she is 23 years old, she makes her first big sale. *Ladies Home Journal* buys her short story "Devotedly, Patrick Henry Casebolt" for $750, and Kerr never again works at a full-time job.

2. The Professional Writer

True ease in writing comes from art, not chance.
As those move easier who have learn'd to dance.

from Alexander Pope as quoted in *Little Little*

In 1993 Kerr was chosen as the fifth recipient of the Margaret A. Edwards Award, given by the American Library Association and *School Library Journal*. With this honor, she joined an elite group of other winners, such as S. E. Hinton, Robert Cormier, Richard Peck, Walter Dean Myers, Lois Duncan, and Judy Blume. Nevertheless, even among the most successful writers for young adults, she stands out as different.

Unlike Paula Danziger, Richard Peck, and Paul Zindel, Kerr never taught high school. In contrast to Judy Blume, Sue Ellen Bridgers, Robert Cormier, Lois Duncan, Norma Klein, and Norma and Harry Mazer, she never had children of her own to inspire her or to act as critics. And unlike Maureen Daly, who wrote *Seventeenth Summer* when she was a college student, and S. E. Hinton, who wrote *The Outsiders* while she was in high school, Kerr wrote her first book from memories of teenage emotions two or three decades old. She was in her mid-forties when Harper and Row published *Dinky Hocker Shoots Smack!*

In spite of these differences, seldom has a writer come to a new field of endeavor with an equivalent background of experience. Kerr had already published five books under the pseudonym Ann Aldrich, over 20 suspense or mystery novels under the names of Vin Packer and Marijane Meaker, and a couple of books as M. J.

12

Meaker. She had also published a few short stories under her "happy pen name" of Laura Winston, and numerous made-to-order confession stories under similarly made-to-order names.

Readers and critics have noted the remarkable fact that Kerr found a new kind of writing, a new audience, so late in life. But in fact, Kerr did not change so much as did the market. Her first breakthrough as a professional author was a short story, a humorous young adult romance entitled "Devotedly, Patrick Henry Casebolt," which she sold to *Ladies' Home Journal* in 1951. At the time, this publication was a prime forum for American fiction writers. Among the contributors to the 1950 and 1951 issues were such notables as Shirley Jackson, Rumer Godden, Jessamyn West, John P. Marquand, and Daphne du Maurier. Kerr was thrilled at selling the story—even when she misread the acceptance letter and thought she was getting $75 instead of $750.

Although the story was published under the pen name of Laura Winston, the subject and the impertinent style are the same as in Kerr's later YA novels. The tale is set in a boarding school much like the one that Flanders Brown goes to in *Is That You, Miss Blue?* The opening is just as unconventional and intriguing as are the leads in Kerr's young adult novels:

> A Paul Jones is a deviation of the old game of musical chairs, only instead of sitting on what you are in front of when the music stops, you dance with it. That was how I first met Patrick Henry Casebolt.[1]

Most of the story is told through the funny letters that the narrator and Patrick Henry Casebolt send back and forth. Patrick Henry Casebolt, "an enormous redheaded, freckle-faced ruffian . . . about to burst out of his gold braided jacket," bears a striking resemblance to *Dinky Hocker*'s 220-pound P. John Knight, "a fat boy . . . nearly six feet, with red hair, freckles and red-apple cheeks."[2] The *Ladies' Home Journal* story is entertaining and fun to read, but of course a five-page short story cannot leave readers with as much to think about as can a 190-page novel.

Nevertheless, if the story had appeared today, an alert publisher might have noticed Kerr's ear for dialogue and her deft touch at comedy and invited her to try her hand at writing a movie or a television script featuring teenagers. Or if it had appeared in the late 1960s, she might have been persuaded to write a novel for teenagers, as was Paul Zindel because of the wonderful dialogue he wrote for the mother-daughter relationship in his Pulitzer prize-winning play, *The Effect of Gamma Rays on Man-in-the-Moon Marigolds*. But in 1951, television was in its infancy, and few publishers were thinking about producing books specifically for teenagers.

Kerr did sell a few teen stories to *Compact*, a short-lived magazine for young people. And Bruce Gould, the editor of *Ladies' Home Journal*, liked "Devotedly, Patrick Henry Casebolt" so much that he came to New York to talk with Marijane Meaker, who he thought was Laura Winston's agent. He wanted to see if Winston would consider moving to Philadelphia and working with a new column that the magazine wanted to start for young people. The history of young adult literature might have been different if Kerr had accepted, but she declined mainly because she did not want to leave New York City. However, during the conversation, she confessed that she was both Marijane Meaker, the literary agent, and Laura Winston, the 23-year-old author of the story.

Gould regarded Kerr's double role as so interesting that he decided to use it in a publicity campaign for the magazine. He arranged for Kerr to be interviewed on several radio shows, one of which was conducted by the well-known Mary Margaret McBride. Dick Carroll, an editor at Fawcett Publications, was listening and heard Kerr say that one of the nine menial jobs she had been fired from during the preceding year had been as a reader at Fawcett. He contacted her and asked if she would be interested in writing a book set in a boarding school for a new line of original paperbacks to be called Gold Medal Books. Kerr countered with the suggestion of a book set in a sorority house since she was much closer to that and, in fact, was still living with three sorority sisters transplanted from the University of Missouri to New York City.

Carroll asked for a few chapters and an outline, which Kerr submitted within a few months. He called her for lunch, and, as they taxied to the restaurant, she remembers going under the ramp near Grand Central Station. In that dark tunnel he told her they were accepting the story and advancing her $2,000. In a fitting bit of symbolism, when the taxi emerged into the sunlight of Park Avenue, Kerr was under contract for her first novel. She wrote the book and named it *Sorority Girl*, but her editor preferred the title *Spring Fire* to capitalize on the fame of *The Fires of Spring*, a James Michener novel that at the time was a best seller.

For the 1950s, the book—which dealt with lesbianism in a sorority—bordered on sensationalism. It was an instant paperback success, selling over one million copies in 1952. Now long out of print, it established Kerr as a novelist and provided her with enough money to take a trip to Europe and to move to an apartment without roommates. She moved to a small building (10 apartments in all) on East Ninety-fourth Street, where she lived for eight years.

One of her neighbors was Tom Baird, an art historian who worked at the Frick Museum. They became close friends, and he too began writing. Kerr thinks that one day he looked over her shoulder as she was typing and said to himself, "I can do that." She was still playing literary agent, partly because it was fun and partly because this role made it so much easier to say nice things about her own work. She sold Baird's first short story for him, the only piece she ever sold for a legitimate client. He began by writing for adults but later wrote young adult novels, including the well-received *Walk Out a Brother* and *Smart Rats*. In 1990 he died from a heart attack; Kerr's dedication to her 1991 *Fell Down* reads "Tom Baird was my oldest and dearest friend and this book is to remember him. So long, dear Tom."

Kerr lived in New York City from 1949 until 1973, a period she describes as the best of times. Her working relationship with Fawcett must have been mutually satisfactory because she spent a decade with them, writing mostly suspense stories under the names Vin Packer and Ann Aldrich. She chose that genre because mysteries were the only original paperbacks that had a chance of getting reviewed in the *New York Times*.

Turning from fictional homicide to real-life suicide, Kerr wrote a hardcover book entitled *Sudden Endings* (Doubleday; 1964).

Also published as a Vin Packer paperback, *Sudden Endings* consists of case studies of the deaths of famous people, including Virginia Woolf, Ernest Hemingway, Hart Crane, Marilyn Monroe, and Joseph Goebbels. Kerr was disappointed that her editor would not let her conjecture beyond the facts she uncovered. She was also surprised at the number of errors she discovered in the galley proofs. These two things convinced Kerr to stick to fiction. However, she says she is still occasionally tempted to undertake a dual biography of fascinating people such as Kate Smith and Bobby Fischer, who were both obsessive but in entirely different ways.

In 1967 Kerr published under her own name what she laughingly called the "obligatory family novel that every young writer must get out of his or her system." She says it was a "terrible bomb called *Hometown*," which appropriately got the most attention in upstate New York, where her relatives were busy expunging it from libraries and bookstores.

When Kerr was about to conclude that her name was a jinx, she published a hardback under the name of Meaker with Little, Brown: *Shockproof Sydney Skate*. This story featuring a teenager became a Literary Guild alternate and a selection of the Book Find Club. The money from the paperback sale enabled Kerr to begin thinking of buying her own house outside New York City.

While living in the city, Kerr also took courses at the New School, studying psychology, literature, political science, sociology, anthropology, and, of course, writing. As a student, she met famous New Yorkers, including Margaret Mead, and made friends with people she would not otherwise have had access to as a neophyte writer. Her friendship with professor Martha Wolfenstein played a pivotal role in Kerr's developing talent. A psychoanalyst specializing in children and young adults, Wolfenstein encouraged Kerr to read Freud, Reik, Stekel, Kubie, Mahler, and Fromm and to subscribe to psychology journals. Without identifying her patients, she talked with Kerr about many of their problems. Through this formative framework, Kerr's Vin Packer books became "whydunits" instead of "whodunits," and she continued to include young people in many of her stories.

Kerr's favorite childhood picture is this drawing by her late friend Louise
Fitzhugh, who based it on a baby photo of the young Marijane.

She liked to fictionalize actual crimes—for example, the Emmet
Till "Wolf Whistle" murder of a young black boy in Mississippi.
Although her stories were intended for adult audiences, she told
several of them from a teenager's viewpoint. In the 1960s another
good friend kept reminding Kerr of this while encouraging her to
try writing for young people.

This friend was Louise Fitzhugh, author of the ground-
breaking children's book *Harriet the Spy*, published in 1964 (Kerr
refers to *Harriet the Spy* as a young adult book, but teachers and

critics are more likely to think of it as an older children's book—something for fourth, fifth, and sixth graders). *Harriet the Spy* brought modern realism to children's literature. Featuring a girl who is intriguing and funny, it disproves the old adage that boys won't read books about girls. The same observations would later be made about Kerr's books, but for a long time Kerr resisted Fitzhugh's suggestion to write for young people because it seemed to her that Fitzhugh was forced to talk down to her audience. Kerr couldn't see herself writing in that limited fashion, but she kept Fitzhugh's advice in the back of her mind and regularly read books written for young people. Nothing clicked until she read *The Pigman* (1968), the book Paul Zindel had written in response to an invitation from Harper and Row editor Charlotte Zolotow. Kerr loved that book and wanted to write one just as good.

Zindel's book, along with such 1967 works as S. E. Hinton's *The Outsiders*, Robert Lipsyte's *The Contender*, and Chaim Potok's *The Chosen* ushered in a golden age of books for teenagers. Teachers, librarians, publishers, critics, and students of young adult literature now look back nostalgically on the 1970s when:

- Federal dollars were available to support public and school libraries.
- Children of an affluent society could afford to buy their own paperback books, and many of them did so in the new chain bookstores that flourished in neighborhood shopping malls.
- Youth-oriented media, especially film and TV, provided new markets for stories about young people.
- Student demands for "relevance" meant that, instead of assigning a whole class to read such traditional works as *Silas Marner* or *Julius Caesar,* more teachers allowed high school students to make selections from lists of contemporary books.

Fortunately for Kerr, all this was happening at about the same time that she was growing tired of murder and crime and becoming more interested in seeing "the light *and* the dark." Reflecting on her life, she came to the same observation that James Thurber once made: Tragedy plus time equals comedy. She sat down to make notes for possible stories. Things that had happened long ago came back to her clear as a bell, "still ringing,"

> Making me smile and shake my head as I realized I had stories in me about *me*—no longer disguised as a homicidal maniac, or a twisted criminal bent on a scam, but as the small town kid I'd been, so typically American and middle class and yes, vulnerable, but not as tragic and complicated as I used to imagine. (*SAA,* 151)

When Roger Sutton asked Kerr how she managed to put herself in the mind of a 14-year-old while at the same time retaining her adult perspective, she said that "One great advantage I have is that I don't live with kids, so I don't have my car coming home wrecked and I don't have to listen to that music that I do love, but not at the decibels they play it." Not having children means that the only childhood she has to keep track of is her own. She thinks that if she had children, her own memories would probably get "a bit fogged over."[3]

Touched by the social turmoil of the sixties, especially the death of Martin Luther King Jr., Kerr wanted to contribute to improving social and educational conditions for African Americans. She began serving in an experimental writers-in-the-schools program. One day a month she would go to Commercial Manhattan Central High School on Forty-second Street, where she would endeavor to pique her English-class students' interest in writing. The students split their days evenly between work and school. She says, "They were wild, unruly, wonderful kids who didn't give a fig for reading, but who responded to writing assignments with great vigor and originality." As part of the program, the students' stories and poems were published in a mimeographed magazine. The most popular writer was an obese girl nicknamed Tiny, who wrote imaginative, grotesque stories. In one of them, a woman went swimming in the Hudson River, accidentally swallowed some strange eggs that were in the water, and subsequently gave birth to a mass of red snakes.

Kerr soon received a visit from Tiny's mother, who complained about Kerr encouraging her daughter to write "weird." As Kerr talked to the woman, and over the next few months as she got to know Tiny better, she found that Tiny's mother spent most of her time aiding drug addicts at her church. Every afternoon Tiny would go home to an empty apartment where she would eat snacks and watch television until her mother came home for supper. After dinner, which was the highlight of Tiny's day, the mother would go back to the church, and Tiny would again watch television and eat until she fell asleep. She was becoming enormous. Kerr says the mother was completely unaware that, while she was putting out the fire across the street, her own house was burning.

Inspired by this mother-daughter relationship, Kerr wrote her first YA novel, *Dinky Hocker Shoots Smack!* Kerr changed the girl's color and her social status to one that she could write about more comfortably, but she retained the basic characters of a do-gooder mother and a daughter desperately in need of her mother's attention.

Kerr offered *Dinky Hocker* to Harper and Row because they had published Louise Fitzhugh's *Harriet the Spy* and because Fitzhugh was enthusiastic over Ursula Nordstrom as an editor who respected writers and their opinions. The company happily accepted *Dinky* and assigned Nordstrom as her editor. When Nordstrom retired, Kerr went on to work with Charlotte Zolotow and then more closely with Robert O. Warren, a man who, she says, deserves much of the credit for her success.

In *ME ME ME ME ME* and other places, Kerr has described the thrill of making her first big sale to *Ladies' Home Journal*. When asked if the publication of *Dinky Hocker* was a comparable pleasure, she responded "Not at all. It was a big disappointment." Editor Ursula Nordstrom had a way of making authors feel excited about whatever they did. Accustomed to receiving between $15,000 and $20,000 for a book, Kerr nevertheless received only $2,000 from the 1972 hardback sales of *Dinky Hocker*. Even though she had already started *If I Love You, Am I Trapped Forever?* she was about to decide that writing for young people was a luxury she could not afford. Then the money from the paperback sale came through, and Kerr was pleasantly surprised to find that "this little indulgence, this sideline" could actually make money.

She combined her profits with those from the paperback sale of *Shockproof Sydney Skate* and moved from New York City to Long Island, buying a house in East Hampton. In spite of what sounds like a bad-luck address—a dead-end street named Deep Six Drive—Kerr's new residence proved to be a good-luck charm both for her and for thousands of young readers. Since 1973, she has happily lived and worked in East Hampton writing books for her youthful audience. The town of Seaville, which appears in so many of her books, is a slightly fictionalized version of East Hampton, just as the town of Cayuta is a fictionalized version of her hometown of Auburn, New York. Some of her most credible characters have been inspired by neighborhood teenagers, and several of her imaginative plots had their beginnings in an incident or activity that Kerr observed from a distance in her new community.

The pleasure Kerr experienced upon discovering that she could earn a living by writing young adult literature must have increased considerably upon ascertaining that she could get ample space in national review media. Being reviewed is an advantage that Kerr values, as shown by the fact that early in her career she wrote mysteries because they were the only original paperbacks that the *New York Times* reviewed. Although Kerr's mysteries were afforded only one or two paragraphs, her YA books began to rate their own headlines. The *Horn Book Magazine*, in an unusual gesture of praise, devoted a whole page to *Is That You, Miss Blue?*, and, when *Gentlehands* came out, the *New York Times* published a four-column review by Richard Bradford. In the June 1977 *Horn Book Magazine*, Mary Kingsbury published one of the first significant criticisms of Kerr as a young adult writer and concluded with:

> Having published five books in four years, Kerr demonstrates the capability for sustained effort that is necessary to achieve a

lasting place in literature. Time alone will determine the longevity of these novels, but it is worth noting that the last two are the best of the five. Short of writing a masterpiece, an author can establish a claim to fame by producing a number of superior books. M. E. Kerr is well on her way to that goal.[4]

In spite of her success, Kerr missed the everyday contact she had had with writers in the city; in East Hampton, therefore, she established a nonprofit writers' workshop in a community center. Participants' fees for the workshop help fund a scholarship for disadvantaged students. Twenty members, including people in their twenties and their seventies, meet once a week for 12-week terms in the fall and spring. Many of the participants enroll over and over as they work on novels. Kerr enjoys the diverse makeup of the group—people whose occupations range from bartender to minister, retired editor, teacher, and realtor.

Having taught this workshop for nearly 20 years, Kerr is now gathering what she and the students have learned about creative writing into a forthcoming book entitled *Blood on the Forehead*. The title comes from the old saying about creative writing being easy: All one has to do is sit there and wait for the blood to form on the forehead. HarperCollins is publishing the book from its trade division, but Kerr thinks it could also be used as a textbook either for advanced high school students or adults in workshops similar to the one she teaches. In keeping with her appreciation for contemporary music, she is including songwriters among the models discussed. She believes that many of today's young people relate more easily to songs than to poems or stories.

During the 20 years that Kerr spent in New York City as a professional writer, she averaged four or five hours a day in suspense writing, which shares some of the characteristics of writing for young adults. Readers of suspense novels are like teen readers in wanting a quick, tight story that they can get into immediately. And because the plots from one book to another are similar, they want the stories enlivened with unusual details and characters. The apparent ease with which Kerr transferred her talents from writing adult suspense stories to writing young adult problem novels with romantic and often humorous overtones may be deceiving; in reality it exemplifies the truth of the Alexander Pope quotation that Kerr had Little Little's English teacher write on the blackboard as encouragement to her students:

> True ease in writing comes from art, not chance.
> As those move easier who have learn'd to dance.[5]

Kerr developed not only skill but also stamina; between 1972 and 1996 no one has matched her record of consistent y popular and critically acclaimed books for young readers.

Ever since the teenaged Marijane begged her parents to let her enroll in the journalism program at the University of Missouri, she has taken a professional approach to the writing and the marketing of both her manuscripts and her finished books. Although some authors assume that they have two or three pages in which to interest a browsing reader, Kerr does not give herself this luxury. She took a class in headline writing for advertisers solely to help her create titles that would catch readers' eyes. She is one of the few authors whose titles are so involved that they need punctuation. She is also one of the few who asks intriguing questions, such as *If I Love You, Am I Trapped Forever?* and *Is That You, Miss Blue?* Sometimes she employs a title to clarify a book's theme, as in *I Stay Near You*, which explores family ties, and *I'll Love You When You're More Like Me*, which shows how emotional attachments are influenced by people's expectations of others.

In 1972, *Dinky Hocker Shoots Smack!* was an especially startling title because the public had become alarmed for the first time over teenage drug use. The title seemed so blatantly sensational that people had to stop and take a second look; they wondered why a respectable company like Harper and Row would publish such a book and why junior high librarians and teachers would endorse it. Their reaction was understandable, for the way in which the title represents the story resembles the misleading ways authors of "true confessions" stories—a trade not unknown to Kerr—attract their readers.

Later when Kerr went out to talk to high school kids, she learned something that the advertising classes never taught, which was that boys were shy about being seen with romantic-looking books that had the word *love* in the title. At least this was the teacher's explanation when boys in one school stood in line to get Kerr to autograph books that had their covers torn off. An alternate explanation might be that the teacher had somehow managed to get "remainder" copies (On mass market paperbacks, bookstores need to return only the torn-off covers to get a refund on books that haven't sold). But either way, not since the 1984 *Him She Loves?* has Kerr included the word *love* in a title. Prior to that she had *If I Love You, Am I Trapped Forever?*, *I'll Love You When You're More Like Me*, and *Love Is a Missing Person*.

Kerr has a running feud with her publishers to keep them from putting pictures of children on the covers of her books. Anything that makes a book look like it is intended for 11- or 12-year-olds cuts down on the readership among the 13- to 16-year-olds that Kerr typically writes for. This includes jacket illustrations, the location of the book in a library or a bookstore, or merely a mention that the book is "children's" literature. Kerr quite rightly observed that "No twelve-year-old minds reading a book that looks like the characters are seventeen, but no seventeen-year-old wants to read about twelve-year-olds."

In spite of the fact that authors are "usually barely tolerated in any discussion of packaging," Kerr designed the cover herself for the hardback edition of *Little Little*. Not wanting readers to prejudge the characters based on a drawing of them, she used the title repeated in black-on-silver block letters in increasingly smaller sizes. She did not have as much influence with the paperback publishers who, she said, feel strongly that to be successful a cover must have an illustration. She has been happier with the way her books look in their foreign editions where she has "seen everything from Red Grooms' 'City Boy,' as a cover for *Fell* (L'École des Loisirs) to a marvelous, almost surrealistic interpretation of *Gentlehands* (Fluwelen Vingers) for Lemniscaat, Dutch."

> Here in the states all YA books look alike, with illustrations that seem to be in a time tunnel of the forties and fifties slick magazine era. They are not art, nor even an attempt to be sophisticated graphic art. Compare them with the jacket art of album covers (reduced for CD's), the stylized presentations on MTV, even video sleeves for popular movies, and these photogenic young people seem more like a page from the Crew or Bean catalogs advertising sweaters and pants.[6]

When asked if she feels pressured to write a book a year, Kerr says no; rather, it is a pace she has set for herself. She never takes advances and so is not obligated to anyone. In answer to the question of how long she can go on without repeating herself, she laughingly acknowledges that she constantly feels on edge, like a guest at a dinner party struggling to tell an interesting story and being nagged by doubts: Have I already told this story to this audience?

By the early 1990s, market conditions for YA books had changed considerably, with the result that some well-established publishers as well as many of the newcomers who had jumped into the YA market during the heyday of the 1970s and early '80s found themselves squeezed out. As the bottom line became increasingly important, many companies began keeping profits close to home by publishing both hard- and softcover editions. Thus, the big dollars for paperback rights that had been such a happy surprise for Kerr with *Dinky Hocker* were no longer available.

These changing conditions gave Kerr the courage to take a new step in her career. She began writing for the younger audience that her friend Louise Fitzhugh had first suggested back in the 1960s. Although she stayed with HarperCollins for her YA books, including the very successful *Deliver Us from Evie*, she began writing easier books for Scholastic, which has a huge school marketing program. She was so apprehensive about whether she could do this kind of writing that she pulled out one of her old tricks and published the first two under the pseudonym: Mary James. Only after she received positive reviews did she agree to identify Mary James as "also known as M. E. Kerr" on the cover of the 1994 *Frankenlouse*.

The publicity and the reviews surrounding the publication of a new book serve to keep an author's name in front of the public and to inform potential readers about other books they may want to read. The fact that Kerr's young adult books have come from HarperCollins for the past 25 years and that she appears to be well established with Scholastic for her "Mary James" children's books bodes well for continuing publicity. When a new book appears, the back of the dust jacket or an inside page is used to announce awards that previous books have won or to quote complimentary lines from reviews as a hint to readers that they would also enjoy these other titles.

Kerr's biggest surprise in getting acquainted with Scholastic, a mass market publisher, is how much they know about marketing; Scholastic's editors are exceptionally sophisticated in their knowledge of what will sell. In today's market, Kerr can see the need for such skills, but still she worries about losing creativity. She says she has never been able to write to order and is almost superstitious about discussing a book before it is finished. This means she does not respond well when an editor suggests a topic that "will sell." *Shoebag*, her book about a cockroach being turned into a human, was definitely not the kind of book a Scholastic editor would have suggested. Kerr and her new editors were happily surprised, however, when it turned out to be both a profit maker and fun for readers as well as for the author.

3. Five Highly Acclaimed Books

> To give recognition "to those authors whose book or books have provided young adults with a window through which they can view the world, and which will help them to grow and understand themselves and their role in society."

Based on these criteria, M. E. Kerr was honored in 1993 as the fifth recipient of the Margaret A. Edwards Award, sponsored by *School Library Journal* and administered by ALA's Young Adult Library Services Association. This chapter focuses on the four books cited by the selection committee, along with *Deliver Us From Evie*, which in 1994 received unusual acclaim.

In her autobiographical *ME ME ME ME ME: Not a Novel*, Kerr writes:

> What's going on in the world is secondary to what's going on in high school, for in those vulnerable teen years high school *is* the world. There . . . the idea of winning and losing starts taking shape, of being in or out, part of the crowd, or an outsider. . . . There, adults other than parents become role models or enemies or objects of ridicule. . . . And with all that is going on, there are changes going on at home, as kids begin to see things they hadn't noticed before: the way their parents get along, or don't, the way their own brothers and sisters are coping. (*ME*, 75)

This is the raw material from which Kerr fashioned not only the five books discussed in this chapter but also the 15 others that have earned her a place among the most highly touted contemporary writers for young people.

Dinky Hocker Shoots Smack!

Dinky Hocker Shoots Smack! was M. E. Kerr's first book for young adults. It is still her most popular and in some ways her best work. The story begins with Tucker Woolf's father advising him not to tell people he lives in Brooklyn but in Brooklyn *Heights:* "Believe me, Tucker, you'll make a better impression" (*Dinky,* 5). Making a good impression is very important to Tucker's father—which is why Tucker feels especially sorry that his dad was fired.

Tucker's father is a fund-raiser for charitable organizations and small colleges. When he loses his job, the family moves from Manhattan to Brooklyn Heights, and Tucker's mother goes to work as a writer/editor for *Stirring Romances* (Tucker is instructed to say she works for Arrow Publications). The first night in Brooklyn Heights, Tucker finds an abandoned calico kitten hiding under an old Chevrolet. He adopts the cat and names it Ralph Nader in honor of the man "who had done his own time under Chevrolets" (*Dinky,* 6). When the cat turns out to be a female, Tucker drops the "Ralph."

As the weeks drag on and Mr. Woolf does not secure a new job, he becomes increasingly nervous. When he also develops an allergy to cats, Tucker has to give Nader away. In keeping with the local custom, Tucker puts a sign on a tree:

> DO YOU FEEL UNWANTED, IN THE WAY, AND THE CAUSE OF EVERY-
> ONE'S MISERY? ARE YOU TALKED ABOUT BEHIND YOUR BACK AND
> PLOTTED AGAINST? THEN YOU KNOW HOW I FEEL. I AM A CALICO KIT-
> TEN PUTTING MYSELF UP FOR ADOPTION. I HAVE ALREADY BEEN
> SPAYED BY DR. WASSERMAN OF HICKS STREET, AND I AM IN GOOD CON-
> DITION PHYSICALLY. MENTALLY I AM ON A DOWNER, THOUGH, UNTIL I
> CAN RELOCATE. IF YOU KNOW HOW A LOSER FEELS AND WANT TO
> HELP, CALL MAIN 4–8415. (*Dinky,* 6)

Into the picture comes 5'4", 165-pound Susan (known as Dinky) Hocker, who adopts Nader and immediately gives the cat her own problem of overeating. Tucker, who visits Nader at Dinky's house, is worried and depressed at how fat and lethargic Nader becomes. As Tucker's mother observes, "Somehow, you identify with that cat, and I don't see why. You've never been a stray. You've always been loved. . . . Why all the concern over this animal?" (*Dinky*, 7).

Through his concern for Nader, Tucker becomes acquainted with Dinky's family: a successful lawyer-father who pays little attention to his family; one of the most insensitive mothers in all of young adult literature; a cousin named Natalia Line, who has just been released from a school for mentally disturbed teenagers; and various walk-ins that Dinky's do-gooder mother tries to help recover from their addictions and personal problems.

Tucker develops a crush on Dinky's cousin. In order to date Natalia, he fixes Dinky up with P. John Knight, another "fatty" who turns out to have much more in common with Dinky than a weight problem. Everything that Dinky's liberal parents approve of and believe in, P. John makes fun of. Finally they forbid Dinky to associate with him. Life gets worse and worse for Dinky until in desperation she does a terrible thing. While Mrs. Hocker is being honored at a community banquet for her work with drug addicts, Dinky paints the message "Dinky Hocker Shoots Smack" on sidewalks, curbstones, walls, and doors of automobiles. As people file out of the awards ceremony, they cannot help but see the shocking statement.

The attention of the whole town is aroused, as is that of Dinky's humiliated parents. However, it falls to Tucker to convince them that "People who don't shoot smack have problems too" (*Dinky*, 187). He explains that Dinky was not being vindictive, she just needed to be listened to. When Tucker asserts that they have all been thoughtless and cruel about P. John's friendship with Dinky, Mr. Hocker says, "It never amounted to much, after all."

"If it wasn't much," Tucker responds, "it was still all Susan ever had" (*Dinky*, 187).

The book has a moderately happy ending. Tucker is allowed to reclaim his cat when his father finds a new job at half his old salary; at the same time, Mr. Woolf discovers that he was not allergic to cats but rather to being unemployed. Tucker's mother enrolls in law school; Natalia goes back to her special school for the summer, only this time as a helper; and Dinky and her parents go off to Europe for a real family trip. Tucker teases his parents that he is going to start overeating so he can go to Europe, too. They just laugh, however, and say that if he can get fat on his own cooking (he inherited this domestic chore when his mother entered law school), then he will deserve something special.

When Kerr wrote this book, she was living in Brooklyn Heights. Since her apartment was near the courts, she was surrounded by lawyers and their families. This was the impetus for casting Dinky's father as a lawyer and for illustrating Mrs. Woolf's ambitions by having her go to law school. Kerr reported that she watched dozens of such women go by her apartment building on their way to Brooklyn Law College. They were "much longer in the tooth" than typical college coeds and were obviously weighed down by family responsibilities as well as by their law books.

The contrast between Tucker's mother and Dinky's mother exemplifies one of Kerr's favorite techniques: setting up contrasting sets of characters in order to give readers something to think about. An Arizona State University student described this show-both-sides approach:

> Tucker's parents weren't the perfect, all-knowing "Ward and June" of *Leave It to Beaver* fame nor were they the insensitive, closed-mind types that Paul Zindel created in *The Pigman*. They had a human warmth about them, and they tried—though not always successfully—to communicate with Tucker. They were the antithesis of the Hocker family, where the parents—especially the mother—were so self-centered that at the end of the story I wondered if they really went to Europe for Dinky's sake or if Mrs. Hocker just wanted to get away from all the embarrassment surrounding the awards ceremony.

Another foil is P. John Knight, whose conservatism highlights the conformity of everyone else's liberal attitudes. P. John is admittedly an unrealistic exaggeration, but Kerr nevertheless deserves credit for finding so clever a way to spotlight the ridiculousness of extreme, unbending attitudes.

Considering how difficult it is for a new YA author to attract the attention of editors and thereby get reviewed (in 1972 only *School Library Journal* attempted to review every book it received), *Dinky Hocker Shoots Smack!* took a surprisingly large share of honors while receiving positive reviews in practically every library or school-related publication. The story is well developed, the plot and characters original and interesting, and the dialogue warm and witty. Kerr, who had been a full-time writer for the past 20 years, must have been amused at those reviewers who praised *Dinky Hocker* as an "impressive first book."

What makes *Dinky Hocker* so popular are the wonderfully fresh and believable details: the description of Nader in her "calorie-drugged sleep," Dinky dressed in her father's old tweed vest worn over a T-shirt and with green cotton pajama bottoms and old tennis socks, and the way the Hocker's Christmas dinner progresses from an elegant holiday occasion to a shambles. Most diet-conscious teenagers have used Dinky's rationalizations and tricks, only not to the same extent. Many young people, probably more today than when the book was written, identify with the hard-nosed line that P. John takes, and they smile knowingly at Marcus and the contradictions that he mouths about pot. Because they have relatives who sometimes need help, they are interested in how the families relate to Dinky's cousin Natalia and to Tucker's Uncle Guy. But most of all they are captivated by the lines Kerr puts into her characters' mouths, such as when P. John predicts Dinky's breakdown by wryly commenting that "fish die belly-upward, too" (*Dinky,* 175) and when Tucker explains that *ass* is a bad word because when "they made the rules, they decided any part of your body that isn't supposed to show isn't supposed to be called by a slang name" (*Dinky,* 154). Young readers are also drawn in by Tucker's false "true confession" that his mother had contrived for her magazine about the hospital nurse who for 20 years had switched around the newborn babies in her care.

The weaknesses in *Dinky Hocker Shoots Smack!* stem from the same source as its strengths, which is Kerr's exuberance. Her

exaggerations make for entertaining reading, but it is a bit hard
to believe that Dinky would or could have painted her message so
that it showed "no matter what street you turned down" (*Dinky*,
177). If she had really painted it on car doors as well as sidewalks
and walls, then the dire consequences should have at least been
mentioned.

Credibility is also stretched by the interrelationships of the cast
of characters. Certainly people as troubled and as eccentric as
each of Kerr's characters exist in real life, but they seldom connect with each other. Having them contribute to solving each
other's problems results in an ending that is a bit too pat. Nevertheless, readers are left with new ideas about schools, family relationships, emotional disturbances, women's roles, and controlling
one's appetites, whether for food or drugs.

When *Dinky Hocker* was presented as an ABC *After-School Special*, its popularity was boosted tremendously, Kerr believes,
although critics were not as kind to the 1978 television produc-
tion as they had been to the book. Kerr had pushed Mrs. Hocker's
characterization to the limits of credibility in the book, and when
the television producers were forced to reduce a 198-page book to
a 35-minute show, they nudged her over the line. However, it was
the role of Nader the cat that bothered Kerr most of all. Kerr saw
the film the one time it was aired and remembers being terribly
disappointed because the producers cast a skinny kitten in the
role, whereas Nader's obesity is crucial to the plot. Kerr believes
they should have used Morris, the famous Purina Cat Chow
model. The book's anti-junk food message also caused trouble
during the television adaptation. Among the original sponsors
were candy manufacturers who backed out after viewing the film,
which may be one of the reasons that it was never broadcast as a
rerun. (The film has been released by Learning Corporation as a
video for school use.)

Such complications are typical of attempts to change books into
films or television productions and are one reason that Kerr does
not see herself participating in similar joint ventures. Writing a
book is something an individual can do basically alone, but
dramatization requires a team effort. Nevertheless, Kerr acknowl-

edges the potential power of the mass media in helping authors woo their readers.

Gentlehands

Kerr jokes about having a captive audience because students sometimes write and confide, as if it were a great compliment, that they were compelled by an English teacher to read one of her books. If a particular title was assigned, chances are that it was *Gentlehands*, which in some respects is Kerr's most intriguing book.

Gentlehands combines a light, entertaining love story with a fairly serious, thought-provoking message. The story starts at the beginning of summer with the kinds of problems that typically beleaguer high school students: the social insecurities of wearing a made-in-Korea Orlon sweater when everyone else sports lamb's wool, falling in love with someone whose pool house is bigger than one's own home, and suddenly seeing one's family through "grown-up" eyes and feeling ashamed.

Sixteen-year-old Buddy Boyle tells the story. He lives "in Sea- ville, New York, on a seedy half-acre lot up near the bay," whereas Skye, the girl he falls in love with summers "on five oceanview acres at the other end of town."[1] Buddy's dad is a police sergeant, whereas Skye's dad is chairman of the board of Penn Industries. Buddy's only previous experience with Skye's social milieu was during a trip with his mother to Montauk to meet "Grampa Trenker," the father she never knew. Grampa Trenker lives in a huge house by the ocean and is "one of these foreign types with the classical music going and a lot of talk about his gardens" (*Gentlehands,* 8). He seemed all right, but Buddy was eager to leave because his mother was so uncomfortable. She had been born in Germany and brought as an infant to the United States by her divorced mother. She resented that not until she was a grown woman had her father even written to inquire about her, and now that he lived only 20 minutes away, she chose for the most part to ignore him. Her explanation for taking Buddy to visit was so that he could see for himself that his grandfather "doesn't have two heads or anything" (*Gentlehands,* 9).

Only when Buddy feels desperate to impress Skye does he think of visiting his grandfather again. Skye invites Buddy to a party at her house, and afterward she surprises him with a kiss "just for the sweetest, shortest time." Then she steps away and touches a button to the garage door, which rolls open so the lights display six sleek cars, including a Rolls Royce and a Jensen. Skye moves toward the Jensen, which she calls "The Jenny," and asks, "Want a lift somewhere, sailor? . . . Make it someplace special, Buddy" (*Gentlehands,* 18).

Buddy amazes himself by confidently saying "Montauk" and then explains that his grandfather lives there. Skye gives this surprise her ultimate compliment: "Oh Buddy, that's subtle! I'm going to like you, Buddy Boyle, I can tell" (Gentlehands, 18).

The visit is such a success that both Buddy and his grandfather acknowledge—and Skye probably recognizes—that Buddy is "borrowing glory" by letting this sophisticated and elegant old man make the impression on Skye that Buddy should have been making with his own personality. But as Buddy philosophically shrugs, "Thank God I had someone in my family to borrow glory from" (*Gentlehands,* 26).

By the end of the book, this borrowed glory almost turns into borrowed infamy when it is revealed that Buddy's grandfather was a Nazi war criminal and that his wealth came from the melted-down gold teeth and jewelry of Jewish victims. Kerr does not try in this 135-page book to answer the questions about the Holocaust that the world has been struggling with for the past 50 years. What she does instead is to make readers wonder about good and evil and what outside appearances impart about inside courage and beliefs.

Of all of Kerr's books, *Gentlehands* was the easiest to write. Upon moving to East Hampton, Kerr lived next door to a 17-year-old boy having his first love affair with one of the wealthy girls whose families spent their summers at the shore. The boy had just gotten a new 10-speed bicycle, whereas the girl had a new Porsche. She had gone to boarding schools in Europe, whereas he had attended the local high school. He would come to Kerr for advice on what clothes to wear and which fork to use first, agonizing over a hundred little details he had never thought about before.

That same summer Kerr was reading Howard Blum's book *Wanted: The Search for Nazis in America*. Blum's book and the experience with her neighbor came together so naturally that Kerr said it took only three weeks to write *Gentlehands*. She was not making the same kind of statement that Mrs. LaBelle (a character in *Little, Little)* makes when she brags about writing her perfectly dreadful poem in a single afternoon. Instead, Kerr was marveling over a phenomenon that she hardly understood. She said it was as if she had a tape recorder in her head, and all she had to do was transcribe the story that someone else had put there.

Gentlehands immediately became controversial. Some critics said it was anti-Semitic because the Nazi—Grandpa Trenker— was much more appealingly portrayed than the Jewish writer who was devoting his life to hunting Nazis. Others claimed that Trenker's switch from villain to hero lacked verisimilitude, whereas still others asserted that the topic was inappropriate for young readers. Kerr was not surprised at the controversy; she had purposely set out to jar people's thinking. "Actually," she said, "Vietnam was as much in my mind as was World War II. As Americans we were in Vietnam, and I kept wondering were we all good people? Is evil conducted by someone next door or by someone so distant we don't recognize them?" She went on to say, "The fact that the boy turned his grandfather in was enough of a lesson to me," but later she wondered if she should have been more specific. She was disappointed when she visited a school in Ohio where the students conducted a trial for Gentlehands and let him go under the philosophy of forgiving and forgetting.

This was not the point Kerr was trying to make. Although we distance ourselves from evil by stereotyping the enemy as buffoons (as in *Hogan's Heroes,* a sitcom set in a German POW camp) or as animals, as in old Japanese war movies, in reality evil lives close to home. Mystery and suspense writers illustrate this fact by so portraying wickedness that for most of the book readers do not know which character is the villain. In this kind of story, the authors ultimately "deliver judgment and do something to the evil character." Kerr now wonders if she should have done the same in *Gentlehands* (Sutton, 26).

Gentlehands is among the most widely read of Kerr's books partly because it fits into course units on Holocaust literature, a popular reading topic in social studies and English classes. At 135 pages, *Gentlehands* may be the shortest book on a teacher's suggested reading list, and, for young readers who have never thought about the Holocaust, it is probably the easiest to accept. The critic who labeled the book a "slick little tale in which the Holocaust and Nazi exterminators become cheap devices to move the plot forward"[2] was looking at the book from the wrong end of the telescope. Kerr's intention was to use the romantic elements to cause readers to think about questions of cruelty and justice. She was following the well-established educational principle of starting where kids are and then progressing gradually to higher levels of understanding.

Kerr's usual strength is character development, but in *Gentlehands* the plot is the most intriguing element. Buddy is the only memorable character; the others border on caricature. If, after the excitement of the three-week writing marathon, Kerr had gone back and further developed the main characters, she might have interrupted the straightforward flow of the story. Nevertheless, *Gentlehands* might have been a better book if Kerr had revised a few of the plotting devices she relied on in her rush to get on with the story. For example, the ending is weakened by Buddy's return to his grandfather's house to find "things strewn everywhere, as though someone had been on a frantic search for something" (*Gentlehands,* 180). Books and tapes were out of the cases; drawers emptied onto the Oriental rug; cups, dishes, and silverware spread out on the kitchen floor; drapes torn from the windows; and wall pictures either crooked or taken down. When Buddy comes in and surveys the destruction, he hears what he thinks is music and a closet door closing.

Supposedly all of this damage, as well as the humanlike sounds, come from a pet raccoon that went wild when it felt abandoned by the now-absent Grandpa Trenker. Buddy doesn't know about the raccoon and thinks that his grandfather must be in the bedroom. He intends to call out, "Grandfather, it's me" but surprises himself by saying "Gentlehands?" (*Gentlehands*, 182).

The significance of this Freudian slip—which shows that Buddy now accepts his grandfather's identification as the Nazi war criminal infamously known as Gentlehands—is obscured by the emphasis on the raccoon. Readers are not ready to concentrate on this subtle and thought-provoking climax if they are still arguing in their own minds about whether a raccoon could do some—but surely not all—of that damage.

ME ME ME ME ME: Not a Novel

Although *ME ME ME ME ME* is not a novel, it is not exactly an autobiography, either. What Kerr offers are incidents or periods from her youth (early teens through her twenties). Some are presented as short stories, whereas others are more like chapters in an autobiography. As she says in an author's note, the book "is an answer to many letters from kids wanting to know if the things I write about really happened to me." If this had been Kerr's first YA book instead of her tenth, there would not have been any readers asking her questions nor would there have been the fascinating fictional characters for her to connect to the real life acquaintances.

The obvious assumption is that students who have read and enjoyed Kerr's previous books will be the readers of *ME ME ME ME ME*, but the reverse may also occur. Readers may happen onto it and become intrigued enough to look for Kerr's novels. As an addendum to each chapter, Kerr includes specific connections between the people she tells about and her fictional characters. Readers not familiar with her novels can easily skip these explanations; few will, however, because they have a verve and style of

their own. For example, Kerr recounts going back to her hometown and having a disillusioning conversation with a man who
used to be her boyfriend, the one on whom she based Wally Witherspoon in *I'll Love You When You're More Like Me*. She concludes,

> My old pal Thomas Wolfe is wrong.
> You *can* go home again.
> You should.
> It gives you lots to think about. (*ME*, 34)

One reason that *ME ME ME ME ME* was so appreciated when
it appeared is that, as the years went by and Kerr tried to keep
from telling the same story over and over again, she created
characters further and further removed from average teenagers
with average problems. She began with ordinary enough Tucker
and overweight Dinky Hocker but from there went on to create
characters whose problems were much more exotic and much
less believable. Writing stories based on her own life forced Kerr
to come back from the fringes of teenage experience and focus
on knowledge that is common to a vastly larger body of young
people.

The only story in the book that does not ring quite true is her
account of movie-star worship in which she and a 10-year-old
friend conspire to obtain a letter from actor Ronald Reagan.
When Marijane writes him that she is crippled and that she went
to see *Brother Rat* in a wheelchair, he responds. Although the
event may have happened, it is a bit of a coincidence that out of
the hundreds of actors starring in 1940s movies, the one actor
Marijane and her friends should have cared the most about was
the one destined to become the future president.

ME ME ME ME ME is read mostly by young women who are
slightly older than her other readers; as they nostalgically look
back on their own childhoods, they can enjoy the lighthearted fun
of the early stories while also appreciating the more serious con-
tents of the later chapters. The book has a staying power that
caused HarperCollins to reissue it in 1994 with a new cover fea-

turing photographs to communicate its autobiographical nature. Arthea Reed recommended the postscripts at the end of each chapter for showing "how personal experience can become the basis for a work of fiction."[3] She predicted that English teachers would welcome contemporary illustrations from a writer whom young readers respect and enjoy. Nancy Hammond, writing for the *Horn Book Magazine,* compared Kerr's *ME ME ME ME ME* to Jean Fritz's prizewinning *Homesick,* which was set in revolutionary China. Hammond complimented Kerr for describing "with drama, humor, and perception a youth less exotic but no less entertaining and compelling" than Fritz's. She also congratulated Kerr for being as appealing in real life as are the "smart-mouth" tomboys in Kerr's novels.[4] The number of times that *ME ME ME ME ME* is either quoted or referred to in chapter 1 as well as throughout this volume reflects strong agreement with Hammond's positive assessment.

Of all of Kerr's books, this is the one that adults are most likely to enjoy reading for their own pleasure. They will especially appreciate the next to the last chapter, entitled "Sorority Life." Marijane started out as a problem pledge by asking such questions as "Why do we have to swear we're members of the Caucasian race when we take the sorority oath of allegiance?" and "Why don't we ever have exchange dinners with Jewish fraternities?" (*ME,* 185). But more interesting than this running tension with the values of sororities and fraternities is her relationship with George, an older student originally from Budapest. Interned for a time in a concentration camp, George subsequently escaped to Venezuela, where he won a scholarship to study in the United States. As he introduces himself to Marijane, he explains that he is from "the Pest side" of Budapest and intends to "become a pest" in her life and make her "think about more important things than Tommy Dorsey and sororities" (*ME,* 188).

Marijane joins the Communist party, "the real thing," and with George and other party members travels to St. Louis to meet William Z. Foster, head of the Communist party. George and Marijane go to meetings together and talk and write about politics

Marijane at a fraternity dance at the University of Missouri in 1948.

and love. George is unwelcome at sorority social events, but he is usually too tired to attend anyway since he teaches Spanish at nearby Stevens College and also waits tables two or three nights a week. Marijane's recounting of a May 3, 1948, visit to Columbia, Missouri, by presidential candidate Henry Wallace is especially well told. A crowd of 5,000 turns out to hear—mostly to heckle—the candidate who is supported by the Communist party. Marijane is probably the only person in the whole crowd to be wearing both a sorority pin and a Wallace button. As an introduction to

Wallace, a female faculty member from Lincoln University (an African American school) gives a speech and is heckled from the crowd:

> We don't want her
> You can have her
> She's too black for us! (*ME*, 195)

"Black," in those days, wasn't meant to describe a black; it was meant to ridicule one. . . . Missouri was still a very southern state, and the university did not accept black students. (*ME*, 195)

Somebody shouts "Nigger!" People begin throwing clumps of grass, pebbles, wads of paper, and even rotten tomatoes. Banners suddenly appear: "Go Back to Russia!" and "Wallace Is a Commie!" The jeers continue but are now aimed at Wallace:

> We don't want him
> You can have him
> He's too red for us! (*ME*, 195)

There are more shouts of "Red! Red! Red!" as the police move in. When the disturbance is over and Marijane goes back to the sorority house with her sisters, she hears such comments as "I was ashamed," "That poor colored woman!" "Wallace wasn't saying anything I don't believe in," and "I might even vote for him, just in protest at what happened" (*ME*, 196).

The riot makes national news, and "the next day nearly every professor stopped his class long enough to express outrage at the students' behavior and bigotry" (*ME*, 197). When Marijane expresses similar feelings to George, she is shocked at his response.

> "Wasn't that terrible . . . ?" I said.
> "It was terribly successful," he said. "It was exactly what we wanted. Our chants got everyone going. Mob psychology . . . it never fails. . . . All you have to do in a southern crowd is toss out the word 'nigger' to get the hackles up!" (*ME*, 197)

When Marijane is shocked that the riot had been programmed by George and her fellow Communists, he tells her, "Don't pick. . . . It was a great wictory!" And for the first time, Marijane thinks that "the way he said his v's like w's wasn't all that endearing" (*ME*, 197).

This was the beginning of the end of their romance, but they keep in touch for years. George returns to Hungary and chides her through letters for the actions of her country. For several years in the early 1950s, she does not hear from him. Then, in February of 1957, she is surprised by a letter from a disillusioned man who, with his wife and babies, had fled Hungary to escape arrest for his part in the 1956 people's revolution, which had been suppressed by the Communist government. He was now living 20 miles from Vienna in a refugee home maintained by some "pretty nice people" who happened to be American Mennonites.

Night Kites

Night Kites was inspired by a human drama that Kerr observed from a distance and then tried to imagine being part of it. She saw one of the most prominent families in her town suffer the sadness of having their oldest son—their pride and joy—come home to die of AIDS—what the townspeople called "gay cancer." She wrote the book in 1985 when the medical profession, much less the general public, knew little about the disease. People were searching for information primarily about the physical aspects of the disease and only as an afterthought about the emotional effect on patients and their families. Although a couple of television programs and off-Broadway plays had touched on the subject, *Night Kites* was the first novel on AIDS written for either adults or teenagers. Kerr did not anticipate playing this kind of a historical role. Because she had every confidence that the medical profession would find a cure for AIDS, she in fact thought the book would soon be dated. Had she been able to foresee the future, she now says, she would have addressed safe sex and condoms. Furthermore, she probably would not have allowed herself the luxury of incorporating references to pop music. Although she has always loved this aspect of teen life, she has mostly steered clear of writing about it because it changes so rapidly.

Because of the drama and the newness of the situation, when *Night Kites* came out the subject of AIDS received most of the attention, as discussed in chapter 8. However, several other aspects of the story also deserve to be looked at. The narrator is 17-year-old Erick Rudd, who has always idolized his brother Pete, 10 years his senior. The title comes from the time that Pete made a night kite for Erick complete with tiny battery lights. As they flew it on the beach, Pete explained that "night kites are different. They don't think about the dark. They go up alone, on their own, and they're not afraid to be different." This is the symbol of the book. Although Erick is "a regular day kind" of kite, Pete is a night kite, and so is Nicki, Erick's on-again, off-again girlfriend.[5]

Nicki—a Madonna look-alike—is one of the most unusual protagonists in YA literature. Although there are plenty of girls in real life who aspire to be like her, authors seldom portray them as fully developed or sympathetic characters, perhaps because the readers of YA literature are more likely to resemble Dill, Erick's first girlfriend. The relationship between Dill and Nicki is especially well done. Nicki enters the story as the flamboyant girlfriend of Erick's best friend, Jack. The first night that they double date,

> Nicki had her own technique for handling social situations. She ignored Dill totally. Dill was directing conversations at her, and saying her name at the beginning and end of every sentence, to make her feel included. . . . Nicki looked right past Dill to me. Nicki spent the evening featuring Jack and me. . . . She was the type who could make a seductive number out of passing you a plastic fork. Her fingers found yours at the same time her eyes did, and both of them caressed you. It was that sort of thing all night. (*Kites,* 7)

The closer Erick and Nicki get, the further alienated Dill and Jack feel. And the longer Erick goes with Nicki, the less he understands her. When they go to the senior dance at which he is going to present Nicki with his senior ring, he dreads confessing to her that "Way back in September, when the seniors had ordered their rings, I'd ordered mine in Dill's size, as a surprise, with Dill's initials and mine inside." Erick is shocked when Nicki responds by clapping her hands together and saying "she just *loved* it, couldn't wait to wear it now!" (*Kites,* 186) But when they get inside the school gym, Dill is the one passing out the numbers for the couples' places in the Grand March. Upon receiving their position, Nicki wants to go home because she is sure Dill purposely gave them number nine with its mystical portents of ill fortune. Erick disagrees not because Dill is above such pettiness but because "Dill knew as much about mystical numbers as Nicki knew about slumber parties" (*Kites,* 189). While Erick is waiting in line for their number, Nicki disappears into the crowd. Dill sees him looking for Nicki and says, "She's lighted on Roman now, up by the dance stand." Erick shrugs and tries to be lighthearted by responding "You make her sound like a mosquito."

> "More like a flea," Dill said coldly. "Mosquitoes glide, almost gracefully. Fleas hop. From person to person."
> "Well, Dill," I said, "you haven't lost your bite, either."
> "I haven't *lost* anything, Rudd." said Dill. "You'll be the ninth couple." She handed me the ticket. (*Kites,* 188)

If there is a lesson to be learned from Kerr's contrasting portrayals of Dill and Nicki, Kerr leaves it to her readers to figure out. For her, it is enough to shine a spotlight on such differences and to illustrate them with a myriad of unusual and believable details.

An additional strength of the book is the manner in which it shows how families react to stress. Near the end of the book, Erick's words, "We're going to hang together. Family is first" are so credible that Pete asks, "Why the hell do all of Dad's old chestnuts suddenly sound good to me?" (*Kites,* 212). But for most of the book, rather than banding together to stave off a hostile outside world, the Rudd family members quarrel with each other. They are all looking for someone or something to blame. They are on edge when Mr. Rudd's parents decide against coming for Christmas, and Mr. Rudd is irritated that the family minister comes on a regular basis to play backgammon with Pete. He complains, "that was a great idea Mom had to tell Snore [the minister], just like her, just like her!"

> "I told Snore!" Pete said.
> "Don't cover up for your mother!" Dad insisted.
> "If Mom *had* told Snore, why would it be just like her?" I wanted to know.
> "Just like her to involve the community in our private affairs!" Dad said. "Just like her now, to let you and Pete lie for her!"
> We couldn't seem to convince Dad she hadn't lied, so I finally just tossed in, "Well, we're all a little mendacious lately, aren't we?" (*Kites,* 184)

Erick had been reading *Cat on a Hot Tin Roof* for English and had picked up the word *mendacious* from Big Daddy's speeches. Fond of the sound of the word, he added that "mendacity" was becoming their way of life; for this impertinence, his frustrated father gave him "a crack across the head. First time ever" (*Kites,* 184).

Kerr ends the book with Pete reading to Erick the beginning of a story that he has written entitled "The Sweet Perfume of Goodbye?" It is about a planet where there are no smells except in the year before death.

> " 'When I woke up this morning, there was a faint fragrance in my room, so subtle and exquisite, I marvel at it. And I know its meaning, but not its pain yet. That will come, for I am changing.' " Pete stopped and looked up at me. "That's not quite right. It should probably read, 'That will come, for I am bound to change.' "
> "He isn't really changed yet," I agreed. "He only sees the change coming."
> "Exactly," Pete said. "There's the sweetness first . . . and later on, the end."

Deliver Us from Evie

If the American Library Association had honored M. E. Kerr a few years later, they undoubtedly would have included *Deliver Us from Evie* in their list of significant books. Published in 1994, it received the equivalent of a starred review and placement on the end-of-the-year best book lists from practically every reviewing source including *School Library Journal*, *Booklist*, *Horn Book*, *VOYA*, *Publishers Weekly*, and the *New York Times Book Review*. *Deliver Us from Evie* is a story about the Burrmans, a Missouri farm family consisting of a father, a mother, sons Doug (age 20) and Parr (nearly 16), and a daughter Evie (age 18). Parr is the "loving but conflicted" narrator who is "as finely drawn and memorable" as is Evie.[6]

The question of Evie's sexual orientation is introduced on page one when Parr describes Pig Week at County High. During the first week of school, the transfers from Duffton School are "the pigs" and "the seniors are out to get you. They call 'SOU-weeeee! Pig, pig, pig!' at you, and they put you in a trash can, tie the lid with rope, and kick you around in it."[7] Parr, who is a junior transferring from the local school to the bigger County High School, gets kicked around not only physically but also emotionally when a few of the seniors hang around his locker. After reading his name on the door, one of them says, "Hey, we know your brother. What's his name again?" "Doug Burrman," Parr tells them, but one of them challenges, "Not *that* brother! Your other brother." When Parr protests that he has only one brother, they ask "What about Evie?" (*Evie*, 1).

This is a question repeated over and over during the school year when the Burrmans lose much of their farm to a flood and also come close to losing 18-year-old Evie to community prejudice and ill will within the family. Perhaps one of the reasons the story rings so true is that Kerr has been writing and rewriting it in her head for the past 40 years. As discussed in chapter 8, it is a story that would have meant a great deal to her if she could have read it when she was a teenager.

Although *Deliver Us from Evie* is intended to make readers consider various aspects of lesbianism, it is not limited to that issue alone. Kerr also touches on the challenge of running a small family farm, on the complications of friendships that cross socioeconomic and religious lines, and, more importantly, on family dynamics when one or more players pull out of a carefully structured pyramid. First, the oldest brother, Doug, under the influence of his college girlfriend Bella, decides to be a veterinarian instead of a farmer. Doug brings Bella home to meet the family for the first time on Thanksgiving, and Parr, who is appointed to say grace, includes "a line about keeping our farm safe from harm, hoping it'd go from my lips to God's ears, figuring God would know what I was really talking about" (*Evie,* 15).

When Evie pursues her friendship with Patsy Duff, whose father is the richest man in town and owns the mortgages on most of the neighboring farms—including the Burrmans'—a desolate Parr sees the writing on the wall and fears that by default he will be the one who has to stay home and help with the farm. And, unlike Doug and Evie, he never even wanted to be a farmer. As he explained early on when the family sat down to a big dinner:

> Mom lighted the candles, and we all sat down to eat Elijah, who'd been our last lamb. He'd been in the freezer since summer, when even Evie'd protested his necessary murder. Elijah, we all swore, could smile and was more like a household pet than something you end up eating with mint jelly. . . . I was chewing away on Elijah and telling myself this was more proof I wasn't cut out for farming, because farming was really a lot about killing, even when you kept the livestock to a minimum— you still had to slaughter some poor thing or send it out to someone else to slit its throat. (*Evie,* 30–31)

Mrs. Burrman had invited Cord Whittle to this dinner in hopes of promoting a romance between him and Evie. Cord is about Evie's age and is a good worker, but big brother Doug is relieved that Cord is not invited to Thanksgiving dinner because "He's a real hick, Mom! If Bella got stuck with that dropout, she'd think that's what farmers are like" (*Evie,* 14).

It is no secret that Cord thinks Evie would make a good wife. His attraction for her precipitates the climax of the book in which he convinces Parr to help him hang a sign from the bayonet on the downtown veterans' monument. The sign reads "EVIE LOVES PATSY AND *VICE* VERSA." Cord convinces Parr, who truly loves his sister, that bringing this kind of public attention to the matter will actually help Evie because Mr. Duff will send Patsy away somewhere and then Evie will "snap out of this thing." That at the time they hang the sign both boys really believe such twisted logic shows how frightened many young people are by the mere suggestion of homosexuality.

It is Evie instead of Patsy who leaves town (to be joined later by Patsy), and Parr is forever in Cord's debt because Cord takes the entire blame for the sign. However, there is little time for pondering the matter because heavy rains combine with melting snow to cause severe flooding. "Levees turned to Jell-O. Whole towns swallowed up. Dogs, cats, pigs, and deer clinging to rooftops. Corpses floating by, set loose from graveyards. People living in tents, attics, cellars, cars" (*Evie,* 172). Suspicions, bad feelings, and hostility cannot withstand the force of the mighty Mississippi, and at the end of the summer when Evie comes back for a visit, the Burrmans sit around their table—"an up-ended hog crate in place of the one that had floated off"—they find they can laugh again, even if it is a bit strained. As Evie pulls away in the rented car, she sends her family "a little two-fingered salute," Parr shouts "Tell Patsy hi!" and Mrs. Burrman, who is starting to walk away, turns around, cups her hands to her mouth, and calls out, "Don't you two be strangers!" (*Evie,* 177).

What these five honored books have in common is that they all ask difficult questions. Kerr does not dwell on the issues long enough to sound preachy nor does she provide the answers. However, she tells good stories that leave readers with food for thought as well as a dash of comfort and compassion.

4. Her Larger
Body of Work

Other people may have more talent, perhaps, but I am willing to
work.

from James Joyce as quoted by M. E. Kerr

In an interview with Jim Roginsky,[1] Kerr quoted the line from
James Joyce and added Joyce Carol Oates's reaction: "That's
being a writer. Say no more."

When looking at how much M. E. Kerr has accomplished, even
without counting her writing under pseudonyms, it would be
hard to doubt the truth of her claim that she is willing to work.
Described here in chronological order are the M. E. Kerr books
that, in addition to those discussed in chapter 3, were published
between 1973 and 1996. Because of space restrictions, her short
stories (see the bibliography at the end of the book) are not
described here but may be cited where appropriate to other
chapters.

If I Love You, Am I Trapped Forever?

Alan Bennet goes against his grandfather's advice when he uses a
first-person point of view to write *If I Love You, Am I Trapped
Forever?* His grandfather, who also wanted to be a writer but
ended up running a department store, tells Alan that writing in
the first person is like painting with watercolors—only geniuses

and small children can do it well. Ordinary mortals end up writing self-involved word-salads that no one but relatives will read.

Alan claims it is not really his story he is telling but that of Duncan Stein, a Jewish boy who moves to Cayuta, New York, at the beginning of his senior year. Duncan, whose parents have come to establish a recovery center for alcoholics, is so different that he is given the nickname *Doomed*. During the course of the year he reverses his negative image by founding and editing a newspaper called *Remote*. It is filled with obscure but very romantic stories and want ads that eventually result in Duncan and Leah (Alan's "terrific" girlfriend) falling in love. Alan forms a strong friendship with Duncan's mother, and by spring he is visiting her every Thursday afternoon when Duncan has to stay at school for yearbook staff meetings.

When Alan spends the evening of the junior prom by himself on the beach drinking wine and reading Dostoyevsky while Duncan takes Leah to the dance, he realizes he has more or less traded places with Doomed. Alan writes the book from the pain of the year's experiences, but for the majority of readers his pain is not as interesting as Duncan's success. Most teenagers identify with the underdog and are pleased to see how fast a boy like Alan can topple from his perch and how someone like Duncan Stein can lift himself to the top through cleverness and hard work.

Although applauding Kerr for presenting mothers and sons who actually communicate with each other, one wonders just how credible it is that a woman with Mrs. Stein's problems could concentrate on a friendship with a high school senior, even if she is flattered by his obvious devotion and touched by his broken heart. The story also has several coincidences, which Kerr defends by having Alan argue against his English teacher's advice that for stories to be believable, they must "avoid all life's bizarre coincidences."[2] Fortunately, most of Kerr's readers are so caught up in the story that they do not worry about such details. They are grappling with the bigger question that she forces them to think about: If you have good intentions, is it wrong to turn someone else's world upside down to fill your own needs?

The Son of Someone Famous

After being expelled from yet another boarding school, Adam Blessing is sent to live with his maternal grandfather in Storm, Vermont, where he makes friends with 16-year-old Brenda Belle Blossom. This vulnerable young girl is presented with such poignant believability that a good deal of the teenage Marijane Meaker must live inside her.

Adam's mother died when he was a baby. Brenda Belle's father is a retired veterinarian and an alcoholic. Adam's father is a prominent politician or diplomat, somewhat like Henry Kissinger at the peak of his shuttle diplomacy days. Adam, who has been sent home from numerous boarding schools, explains that he cracks under the pressure to keep up the family image of super success. Scoffing, his father says that is an excuse, not a reason. Adam, who takes his grandfather's name for anonymity, has a crush on Christine Cutler, the most popular girl in school.

Having no chance of going out with Christine, Adam settles for a friendship with Brenda Belle. She thinks it will please her mother if she goes steady, whereas Adam thinks having a girlfriend will help him fit in. Coincidences start piling up when Adam's former stepmother, a has-been movie star, decides to come for Christmas and is recognized by faithful fans, namely Brenda's mother and aunt. She is soon followed to town by a starlet who has been dating Adam's father and wants to become Adam's next stepmother. Adam is the one who has to cope with her suicide attempt when she figures out that his famous father is trying to ditch her. And finally Brenda learns the shocking true story that Adam's natural mother was killed when she was running away with Christine Cutler's father.

Even though in *ME ME ME ME ME*, Kerr makes fun of her mother and her aunt for loving Hollywood gossip, she apparently inherited their interest, as evinced by the number of her books that include show business celebrities as second-level characters. However, their portrayals do not ring true. Mary Burns noted in a review that the "incidents seem patched together from speculation about a life style sensed but not experienced."[3] If it were only Adam's father who was the celebrity, this would not be an issue because he never actually appears. But when his former wife and his girlfriend both arrive in town, the story comes close to disintegrating. Their actions—especially those of the girlfriend—are so clichéd that readers care little about them.

Today, as Kerr looks back on *The Son of Someone Famous* from her experience in streamlining stories for younger readers, she says that even she does not understand all the subplots she introduced into Adam's story. Nevertheless, she deserves credit for at least bringing up a topic that few other writers have dared to broach: a parent's sexuality. Adam is embarrassed at the women his father dates and the snide remarks made in gossip columns insinuating that he is a dirty old man. He is reluctant to criticize because he thinks his father has earned the right to behave anyway he wants, whereas Adam has not done enough in life to have the right to question. Readers know better.

Is That You, Miss Blue?

Is That You, Miss Blue? is an autobiographical novel based on Kerr's experiences at boarding school. Fourteen-year-old Flanders Brown tells the story, beginning with her train trip from New York to Virginia. She meets an "old" student, Carolyn Cardmaker, who feels qualified to expound on everything and everyone. As Carolyn explains, she has a high IQ, and she's also a P. K. (preacher's kid), which means she is a category one student: bright and pitiful. Category two students are girls whose socialclimbing parents like the prestige of having a daughter away at boarding school; category three girls are those who are in the way because their parents are getting divorced or have more exciting things to do than raise children, and those in category four are "out of the ordinary," handicapped or exceptionally bright or beautiful, and so on.[4] Carolyn decides that Flanders is a number three, and midway through the book Flanders almost agrees.

Part of the appeal of this book is that it satisfies some of the curiosity that readers feel as they look forward to moving out of their parents' homes. Flanders "felt a rush of loneliness, the type that comes for a second or two like great punches in the stomach and then goes without doing any damage, except to keep you ever alert to the idea that your life has changed completely, overnight" (*Blue*, 33). Surrounded by strangers she is not sure she will ever care about, Flanders envies Cardmaker because she appears so involved with "everything and everyone." Flanders soon learns, however, that Cardmaker is suffering from misplaced envy—a not uncommon occurrence at Charles School.

Because Flanders has asthma, she is assigned to room with Agnes, who is deaf. They are put in an out-of-the-way dorm so they won't awaken the other girls if they make noises in the night. Miss Ernestine Blue is assigned as the faculty "pal" living on the same floor with them. She is a woman who Flanders senses needs protection. In an article for the *ALAN Review*,[5] Kerr described a high school teacher she had a crush on back in Auburn, New York. Many of this teacher's characteristics are evident in Miss Blue, who, in Flanders's words, "had the effect on most people of embarrassing them, as in the sentence 'I was embarrassed for her' " (*Blue*, 23). In class, Miss Blue is a wonderful teacher, but personally she is as mysterious as the scientific puzzles that she explores with students. She is "only around forty, not old and strange from living too long, but strange for some other reason" (*Blue*, 112). Cardmaker explains to Flanders,

> "She can hear Jesus. Far out."
> "What do you mean she can hear Jesus far out? Far out where?"
> "I mean it's far out that she can hear Jesus. It's Ding-A-Ling City." (*Blue*, 4)

Ambiguous feelings run throughout the book, with Flanders making fun of Miss Blue and then feeling guilt, shame, and protectiveness. When Miss Blue is dismissed from her teaching position—even a church-sponsored school like Charles cannot cope with a teacher who tells students that Jesus has just been in her room—Flanders and her friends conspire to soften the blow for her. But in spite of their efforts, when Flanders gets home for Christmas where everything should be just fine, she suddenly gets "the loneliest feeling in the world," and as her father and grandmother shout "Merry Christmas!" she whispers into the storm, "Miss Blue, are you okay?" She knows the answer is no (*Blue*, 158).

Although today's boarding schools are not as strict as the one that Kerr portrayed, people's inner feelings are much the same, and those are the focus of this story. An apt description by a reviewer for *Best Sellers* explains that what Kerr does is to "dig deep and scurry around in the loneliest, saddest corners of a reader's soul."[6]

Love Is a Missing Person

Love Is a Missing Person has been singularly ignored by the prize givers and is now out of print. This does not mean it is a "bad" book; it is just not quite such a "good" book as some of the others. When Lillian Gerhardt reviewed it in *School Library Journal*,[7] she said it was "as interesting as unfinished gossip." This description hints at the book's weakness as well as its strength. The weakness is that it tries to tell too many people's stories. The strength is that instead of looking at the most obvious aspects of these stories, Kerr zeroes in on aspects that usually stay below the surface.

The idea for the story occurred to her when she went to a high school football game in East Hampton and saw a pretty blonde girl greeted by the cheerleaders in a way that showed she used to be one of them. In her arms, she carried a baby wrapped in a blanket. Standing at some distance behind her was a tall African American boy. As the girl unfolded the blanket for the cheerleaders to see, Kerr caught a glimpse of a tiny brown baby.

When Kerr said something to a nearby friend about the inevitability of intermarriage, her friend responded with, "Ah,

This 1976 picture of Kerr and her dog Irving was taken shortly after she moved from New York City to her own house in East Hampton, New York.

but that's not the real story. The real story is the anger that black girls have" because the white girls are taking "their men." African American sports heroes date white girls, but there is no comparable group of white boys dating African American girls. Kerr tried to bring this insight to a wider audience in *Love Is a Missing Person*.

Kerr is skilled at creating characters with whom readers can identify, but in this book the characters are spread thin. Fifteen-year-old $uzy $lade, whose name is written with dollar signs because of her family's wealth, tells the story. But crowding her off the pages are various relatives and friends. First is her older sister Chicago, "an original" who roars into town on her motorcycle and then charges out again, taking with her the gorgeous African American athlete who was the senior class valedictorian.

He was also, until Chicago's arrival, the boyfriend of Suzy's African American girlfriend and fellow worker at the town library. Suzy's divorced mother and father also appear, and, two-thirds of the way through the book, her father's new wife, a former cocktail waitress named Enid, enters the picture.

A quite separate story is that of Miss Gwendolyn Spring, the librarian who supervises Suzy and her friend. Miss Spring lives in the past, dreaming about her World War II romance with Lester Quinn, who one afternoon appears at the library. Suzy is surprised that he is not "the baby-faced, innocent-eyed, laughing lieutenant" in the framed picture on Miss Spring's desk. He comes to borrow money, which to Suzy's surprise Miss Spring lends him and then explains, "Do you think his wanting a loan could puncture a delusion that has been in existence since the end of World War II?"[8] Later she confides to Suzy, "I wasted myself in futile fantasy. I grew wrinkles dreaming. Wrinkles should come from living, not imagining that you are" (*Missing,* 158).

Miss Spring's story is perhaps the most intriguing in the book, but it is overshadowed by the more recognizable stories of sibling rivalry, interracial loves and resentments, a wealthy older man marrying a sexy young woman he does not respect, and two teenagers rebelling against family and society by running away.

Perhaps Kerr crowded so many stories into what began as an exploration of relationships between black and white teenagers because she was not sure she could write about characters outside of her own experience. She says it is a subject she would still like to explore, but she thinks she will not try to tackle it. She was discouraged when she asked African American author Walter Dean Myers if he had read the book and what he thought about the way her black characters talked. He responded, "Well, they are different" (Sutton, 28).

I'll Love You When You're More Like Me

I'll Love You When You're More Like Me is the story of Wallace Witherspoon Jr.'s life during the summer between his junior and senior years of high school. It begins and ends at almost the same place with Wally giddy with love (and lust) for Lauralei Rabinowitz. On the first page of the book, it is early spring, and he and Lauralei are in the back of the family hearse—Wallace's father is a mortician—and he is whispering "I love you, I love you." Suddenly Lauralei sits up, reaches for her comb, and declares that they cannot continue because Wallace is not Jewish, he is shorter than she is, and he is going to be a mortician. Five months later, on the last page of the book, Wally catches up with Lauralei as she is leaving the school building. During small talk, he learns that she is no longer going with the boy who succeeded him. After she links her arm in his, he grandly announces that he has decided not to become an undertaker.

"Marvelous," she says. "Super. . . . Now if you were two feet taller and your name was Witherstein, you'd be perfect!"[9] Wally does not take her statement too seriously because, as his Uncle Albert says, "You can't win them all." And after what Wally has been through, he knows that anything might happen.

During the summer between Wally's school-year courtships of Lauralei, he finds himself unofficially engaged to Harriet Hren, who is shorter and prettier than Lauralei and who also has some very good ideas for the mortuary business. "But Harriet was a math lesson and Lauralei was a whole course in Chemistry" (*Like Me,* 4–5). That summer Wallace also becomes friends with Sabra St. Amour, a teenage soap-opera star who is suffering from an ulcer and who has come to Seaville for a vacation while the grownups in her life figure out how to keep her both healthy and a star.

In spite of its situation-comedy approach, the book addresses some serious topics: parental pressures, the price of fame, a mother who embarrasses her daughter with her sexual longings, and a likable young man, Charlie Gilhooley, who is Wally's friend and a homosexual. In that part of the story, Kerr manages to walk the thin line between laughing at Charlie and being sympathetically amused at his frustrations, as when Wally asks him how he can mourn the loss of a love he has never had. Charlie retorts, "Try it sometime. It hurts worse" (*Like Me,* 78).

Little Little

Of her early books, *Little Little* is Kerr's favorite, not because it is the best, she says, but because it was so hard to write. "Maybe a parent who's finally raised a particularly difficult child feels this same affection and pride when that kid turns out okay" (SAA, 153). The story was inspired by seeing the golden boy from her hometown go away to Harvard and come back with a wonderful wife. They were everyone's idea of a marvelous young couple, but then when their first child was born, she turned out to be a dwarf. Kerr stood at a distance and watched this carefree couple change into fighters for their little girl, trying to find friends for her and mold her into a happy contributor to society.

Little Little is a romance—a love story of sorts, but with a few extras. The main characters are all dwarfs. They include a beautiful heiress—soon to be 18—and two competing suitors. Little Little is the heiress. Extremely bright, witty, and likable, she is described by her mother as "p. f." (perfectly formed). One of her suitors, however, has a hump on his back and a misaligned tooth; the other suitor has a code of ethics that is somewhat askew.

The book employs alternating narrators, a device Kerr frequently uses so she can write in the first person and still insert the viewpoints of both the girl and the boy. The tale begins with a chapter told by Sydney Cinnamon, the humpbacked dwarf. Seventeen years old, he recounts his life first at an orphanage and then as an upstate New York celebrity who makes television commercials, appears at shopping centers, and stars at openings of bowling alleys and cut-rate liquor stores. Sydney wears a cockroach costume, works for a pesticide company, and has his own theme song, "La Cucaracha," as well as his own groupies: kids who gather at his appearances, waving pieces of paper for autographs.

The second chapter by Little Little La Belle opens with a rhymed invitation, written by Little Little's conventional and somewhat silly mother, to her eighteenth birthday party. After the invitation, the chapter shifts to Little Little's own flip irreverence. Readers immediately see the contrast in background between Sydney's upbringing and Little Little's.

Although the book is one of Kerr's funniest, it is also one of her most serious. Its recurrent theme is people's mistrust of—and sometimes cruelty to—the outsider, the odd person. Kerr cleverly offers several spoonfuls of sugar to make the message go down. For romantics, she offers the love story between Little Little and Sydney, whereas for cynics she offers a chaser of candid and humorous observations. As a further guarantee that the story will not be too harsh, she makes her heroine's problems the kinds that most teenagers would not mind having—for example, deciding between two suitors and being stared at by people who smile as they would at a charming little girl.

Kerr thought Little Little's story would appeal to teenagers because nearly all of them feel somehow different, and the mothers of teenagers are constantly scrutinizing their children's friends and commenting on appearances. That Kerr could use the physical characteristics of dwarfism to discuss differentness in symbolic terms—without sacrificing the feelings of dwarfs— speaks highly of her skill and her sensitivity.

She received letters from dwarfs who read and liked the book, some wanting to know if it would be made into a movie because they wanted to try out for parts. Kerr was surprised when the mother of one dwarf told her that often p. f. dwarfs do not function sexually, whereas deformed dwarfs do. Kerr is not sure that she would have wanted to know this before she wrote *Little Little*.

What I Really Think of You

Years before the scandals involving television evangelists Jimmy Swaggert and Tammy Faye and Jim Baker, Kerr wrote about a romance between the daughter of a small-town Pentecostal preacher and the son of a successful television minister. She has long been fascinated by how parents exert pressure on their children to follow in the family business. In churches the pressure is especially strong because it is exerted in front of, or in collusion with, the congregation.

What I Really Think of You makes readers contemplate both big and little questions of the inner soul. Jesse Pegler is the son of Dr. Guy Pegler (he has an honorary degree from a Bible college), whereas Opal Ringer is the daughter of Pentecostal preacher Royal Ringer—a big, fierce-looking man whose thick black eyebrows meet at a point on his nose. His wife keeps reminding him that he must use his nice smile once in a while or "those little tykes" that come to services at The Helping Hand Tabernacle are going to cry.

The two P. K.'s happen to live in the same town, but there the similarity ends. Jesse helps his father by distributing "It's Up to You" bumper stickers to teenagers at the drive-in sunrise services and by making hospital visits where he passes out the charm of the week and tries to do the helpful little tasks that his father's manager calls "bottom-line Christianity." Jesse is usually accompanied by Seal Von Hennig, the girlfriend that his older brother Bud left behind when he ran away. Jesse doesn't know if Seal really wants to help or if she is just waiting around in hopes that Bud will return. Either way, she makes herself useful by taking notes on those choir members who don't "light up" when they sing and on the need for the television camera to zoom in on more African Americans and Hispanics.

These are scarcely the concerns of Preacher Royal Ringer, whose biggest problem is money. (Of course, Dr. Pegler worries about money, too, but on a different level.) Opal's father's tiny flock is getting even tinier and the weekly offering is hardly enough to pay the church bills, much less support his family. He first blames his financial problems on inflation and then changes his mind: "It ain't inflation . . . it's infiltration."[10] The guilty ones are the outsiders who come right into people's living rooms on television.

The competition between Jesse's and Opal's fathers seems too lopsided to be taken seriously, but then through some rather unlikely events, Dr. Pegler "steals" The Hand's "miracle." In the course of this, Jesse attends a "healing" at The Hand, and for the first time he and Opal see each other. All that Opal remembers about this first meeting is "the sickness back inside me, wanting no part of The Hand, wanting to be anyone but Opal Ringer, embarrassed for myself, the speck of my dream that doesn't know about the glow coming" (*Think,* 35).

Jesse knows that his family is only a generation removed from the kind of preaching that Opal's father now does. He is drawn to her in spite of outward differences such as the fact that he has a new car and designer clothes, whereas Opal waits for rides in her brother's broken-down truck and has mostly hand-me-down clothes that she is afraid to wear for fear they will be recognized by their former owners.

Opal is the most believable and memorable character in the book, probably because she was inspired by a real person. Kerr was drawn into a religious book store by the sounds of wonderful jazz. It was Jimmy Swaggert playing the piano. As Kerr mingled with the crowd, she saw a vulnerable-looking girl standing behind the counter. Her parents owned the store. Some high school students wandered in and spoke to the girl in that mocking tone young people use when they are being cruel. Kerr was fascinated with this girl and the relationship between her and the other teenagers. The store was affiliated with a small church that Kerr visited so she could see the girl interact with her father and mother and with those who came to services and healings. Once, during a 24-hour revival, she saw the girl standing outside distributing literature. Perhaps the strong sympathies that Kerr developed for the girl influenced her to create the wish-fulfilling ending in which the girl sings in tongues and becomes a kind of celebrity.

Television producers offer money and invite Opal to come and sing, but she declines because she belongs to The Helping Hand Tabernacle. To hear her, people must come down to the Hollow. Six months later, Jesse Pegler says "She's the hottest ticket in town. They come from far and wide to see Opal, and hear her sing in tongues" (*Think,* 205).

The strength of the wish fulfillment is not so much that Opal is now a star and her father's church is filled with people, but that the Ringers managed this success without compromising their principles. In contrast, the Peglers are still arguing among themselves about whether Jesus would have used television if it had been available. Frustrated, Jesse decides that he is not going to any church for a while, a decision that his usually sensitive mother dismisses with, "Oh, now *you're* going through that stage" (*Think*, 205).

Him *She Loves?*

During the years that Kerr lived in New York City after graduating from college, she had many Jewish friends and developed a strong interest in Jewish humor and culture. She dated Jewish boys and was surprised to find herself a *goy* and to realize that to a Jewish boyfriend's mother, she did not look so good. "*Her* he loves?" is a phrase from this period that stuck in her mind. Three decades later, she altered it to "*Him* she loves?" which she used as the title for her eleventh YA book.

Kerr made the girl's father a Jewish comedian because she wanted the chance to have fun with Jewish humor. Also she felt that because a Jewish comedian capitalized on Jewish stereotypes, those stereotypes were more likely to be part of the family's life than if the father were a dentist or a teacher.

Henry Schiller tells the story. At 16 he is the youngest of three brothers who, with their mother, have just opened a German restaurant in Kerr's fictional town of Seaville, on the tip of Long Island. They have moved away from bad memories connected with their old restaurant in Yorkville, where Mr. Schiller was killed in a holdup.

The story begins when Valerie Kissenwiser comes into the new restaurant to see if it will be appropriate for her sister's sweet 16 party. As soon as she finds out that the restaurant is German, she explains that she is sorry, she has made a mistake. Her grandmother is giving the party and "we're Jewish. My grandmother doesn't buy Volkswagens or Mercedes. . . ."[11] Henry does not concentrate on the conversation except to understand that Valerie herself "would almost kill for good strudel" (*Him,* 3) and that when Henry starts school on Monday he will probably see Valerie "around."

When Henry sets out to court Valerie, the main complication is that Valerie's father, nationally famous comedian Al Kiss, does not want his daughter to marry a "goy." He forbids their dating, but the restriction only heightens their longing for each other, and they devise creative ways to be together.

Al Kiss's career is not going well; his jokes are tired, and he is no longer considered a fresh young talent. When he is on a talk show, he happens to mention Valerie and his frustration over "*Him* she loves?" The audience laughs. Al Kiss has struck a sympathetic chord in America's parents. He develops a whole new routine making fun of "Heinrich, Sauerkraut Breath." Henry, however, fights back and in a less-than-credible, but psychologically satisfying, series of incidents proves himself a worthy opponent to Al Kiss. And best of all, even though Henry eventually loses Valerie as his girlfriend, he gains Al Kiss as a substitute father. Most high school romances cannot last, and it is refreshing to have Kerr show that life goes on after steadies break up.

The humor and the exaggerated stereotyping of both the Kissenwiser and the Schiller families gives *Him She Loves?* a frothy tone; more than most of Kerr's books, it seems to be written for short-term entertainment. To teenagers from different faiths who are attracted to each other, family objections are indeed a serious matter. But because in *Him She Loves?* the issue seems to disappear, readers do not come away pondering the story with the same seriousness with which they think about the ideas brought out in *Gentlehands*, *Little Little*, and *What I Really Think of You*.

I Stay Near You

Because as a child Kerr never liked to read "historical" books, she has hesitated to write a book set in the 1940s, yet she is haunted by the World War II years and has long wanted to write about some of the effects on young women, whose stories have for the most part been ignored. So that she could write about these years and still not seem too historical, Kerr introduced young readers to the cross-generational novel while still keeping within the two hundred pages that most teenagers prefer. She called the book *I Stay Near You* with the subtitle, "One Story in Three."

The book begins with "Mildred Cone in the Forties," continues with "Welcome to My Disappearance," the story of Mildred's son Vincent Haigney in the 1960s, and ends with "Something I've Never Told You," a Memorex tape that in the 1980s Mildred's grandson, Powell Storm Haigney, is making for his father, Vincent, who by now has become a rock star.

In the 1940s, Mildred lives in the west end of Cayuta near the train tracks, the dump, and the Cayuta Rope Factory. Because she wants to better herself, she learns to play the harp and transfers to preppy East High, where she is at best tolerated. In the summer of 1943, when the boys have gone off to be soldiers, the Cayuta Yacht Club is forced to replace bar boys with waitresses, so Mildred, who by now has blossomed into a buxom beauty, spends the summer carrying drinks to people out on the lawn. On a "picture-postcard afternoon" in late June, the Storms, owners of the Cayuta Rope Factory, dock their big boat at the club. Waitress Mildred and wealthy Powell Storm Jr., the family's only son, have both a literal and a figurative run-in, which is so special that everyone at the club stares, including the Storms. The narrator remembers their beautiful faces frozen in time in what turns out to be the family's last peaceful moment.

Mildred and Powell have a relatively private, but intense, love affair; Powell goes off to the war, never to return; pregnant Mildred marries a tender-hearted boy with a propensity for rescuing creatures in need. True to the genre, Mildred has a son but does not inform the Storms.

In part two, the boy grows almost to adulthood unaware of his relationship to the richest family in town. He falls passionately in love with a girl from the lower classes—in fact, from a criminal family. He is brokenhearted when she rebuffs him.

To shake her son out of his depression, Mildred tells him about his real father. Of course he contacts the Storms, and of course the consequences are tragic. But out of them comes the narrator of part three, Mildred's grandson, who, as a high school senior, tells his story through a tape being prepared as an English class assignment.

Kerr makes Mildred's son a rock musician because popular music is one of her "enthusiastic interests." Nevertheless, Vincent Haigney comes across as the least believable of the characters. He serves mainly as a sounding board, first for Mildred and then for Powell as his intended audience.

The stories are tied together by a gold ring inscribed in the maternal grandmother's Basque language with the message, "I stay near you." Each Storm man is to pass the ring on to his eldest son at maturity. Perhaps the bad luck begins when Powell defiantly gives the ring to Mildred because his family refuses to let him give her a diamond engagement ring. It continues when Mildred's son, not knowing what it is, gives it to his runaway girlfriend. The Storms reclaim it at great trouble and expense, and Mildred's son—in a premature farewell gesture—passes it on to his own teenage son. In part three the bad luck promises to change when Mildred takes charge and, for safekeeping, wears the ring around her neck on a gold chain, just as she did when she was a high school girl in love with its owner.

Fell, Fell Back, and *Fell Down*

After Kerr wrote *Little Little*, she was so exhausted that she wanted to do something less challenging, something that she could fall back on between her serious writing projects; she thus came up with the idea of revitalizing an old talent by writing a mystery series for young readers. She created a likable young man named John Fell, made him the son of a policeman turned private detective—who six months earlier had died of a heart attack while on surveillance duty—and then entangled him in some fantastic but appealing situations. One of those situations is falling in love with the rich girl next door, being "blown away by the kind of passion that made Dante write about Beatrice, Tristram hunger for Isolde, and my father's last client dog the steps of his young, unfaithful wife. . . ."[12]

The main reason Kerr thought that writing a detective series would be easier is that she could rely on the same cast of characters for several books. But writing mysteries for young readers has some unique challenges, one of which is that readers expect a murder in most mysteries. Because readers feel uncomfortable at the prospect of teenagers committing the kind of premeditated murders that make mysteries challenging and fun to read, authors have to be extra clever in creating plots.

In the first book, a wealthy neighbor offers John Fell (who prefers to go by his last name) a chance to attend the exclusive Gardner prep school under his son's name. Fell is told that the son has too many allergies to go to school in a little farm community in central Pennsylvania. Also, the son is afraid of heights, and new students at Gardner have to climb to the top of an on-campus tower. Mrs. Fell is suspicious, especially when she learns that the boy's stepmother is not to know about the arrangement, but the clincher in the deal is that the boy's grandfather has left him $10,000 if he goes to Gardner and another $10,000 if he gets into the mysterious Sevens Club. If Fell assists with the subterfuge, he will get this money plus have his expenses paid.

Fell enrolls in the prep school, whereas the real son goes off to school in Switzerland. All goes well for the first few months, but things start to fall apart when the neighbor and his wife are arrested as spies who have been selling nuclear secrets abroad. The real reason the man had wanted his son to go to school in Switzerland was for safekeeping; he was planning to get out of the spy business and escape from both his wife and the United States government. Fortunately for Fell, by the time all this is uncovered, the money is already in the bank, including the extra $10,000 for being chosen a member of the Sevens Club. All Fell loses in the deal is his fake name and a new girlfriend that he discovers was really the neighbor's 25-year-old lover assigned to "baby-sit" him. He even gets to stay on at school because one of the privileges granted to the Sevens Club is that no member can be expelled.

About two weeks after Fell returns from Christmas break, he sees a crowd gathered down by the tower where a broken body is lying on the pavement.

> "He's committed suicide, Fell!"
> Beside Lasher's body, I saw his thick glasses with the panes smashed.
> Then in less time than it takes a paper clip to inch over to a magnet, I said, "No. He didn't kill himself."
> Those five words were going to get me into a lot of trouble.
> Someday I'll tell you about it. (*Fell,* 164–65)

And of course, that is exactly what he does in *Fell Back*, where the solving of the murder/suicide is only part of the complicated story. The major plot relates to Fell's getting the job of tutoring and befriending Nina Deems, a town girl whose father had been a member of Sevens. As it turns out, this one whiff of privilege and luxury has ruined Mr. Deems because now he will do anything— including drug dealing—to procure for himself the kind of life he thinks he deserves.

Although *Fell Back* was a nominee for the Mystery Writers of America Edgar Award, the book was not as successful with young readers because of the complex plot. Marjorie Lewis, who reviewed the book for *School Library Journal,* said that it "fell short in story" so that readers do "not care at all whether Lasher's death was a murder or a suicide—actually, neither Lasher's beautiful sister, his parents, nor his classmates seem to care much either." What keeps the story interesting is "Fell's personality—his wit, intelligence, and charm. . . . [R]eaders will like him and his insecurities, as they await the next book."[13]

Fell Down has a more intriguing, if still not believable, plot. Again, it is about a man whose life has been influenced by being part of the mysterious Sevens Club. This time it is Lenny Last, a less-than-successful ventriloquist, who comes back to town to perform the Sevens Revenge on Nina Deems's father. After his

gruesome deed, Lenny dies in the same car accident that kills
Fell's best friend. Through some complicated maneuvers, Fell
acquires the journal that Lenny has kept all these years, written
through the voice of "The Mouth," his one-of-a-kind puppet,
which is at the center of a murder mystery nearly three decades
old. Several chapters come from "The Mouth," which is really
Lenny Last's uninhibited subconsciousness. These give Kerr a
chance to write in a tone quite unlike anything young readers are
used to meeting. Lenny was born on September 1, 1945, the very
day the Japanese surrendered. As The Mouth puts it:

> Just when the Japs were crying in their saki as their emperor
> surrendered in Tokyo Bay, Mommy's little sweetums was at
> Lenox Hill Hospital bawling in his crib.[14]

Fell Down ends not only with the mystery on the verge of being
solved but also with Fell putting one of his dad's old detective
friends back in touch with his mother as a possible suitor. For
teen readers, who hanker to control their parents' love lives, this
may be the most wish-fulfilling part of the series.

Kerr was surprised when a newspaper reporter called to interview her from Missouri where he said that a local school board
was asking that all the *Fell* books be removed from district
libraries because they were "supporting suicide and the occult."
She was astonished for two reasons. First, as mysteries go, the
Fell books "are *so* innocent," and second, having gone to school in
that state, she feels a special affinity for the area. She wisely prac-
ticed restraint, however, and kept the mischievous part of herself
from telling the reporter that everything she knew about the dark
side of life she had learned at the University of Missouri.

Linger

Although *Linger* is, on the surface, a story about the Gulf War, it
is actually about prejudice at home. Sixteen-year-old Gary Peele
tells the tale of his brother's falling out with Mr. Dunlinger,

owner of the Linger Restaurant, and joining the army to get away. The Linger Restaurant is the center of Berryville's social life:

> It wouldn't seem like Christmas in our town without the Linger tree [and the] carols every December fifteenth. . . . Easter there was the egg rolling out on the lawn, for the kids . . . and on the Fourth of July, Linger's fireworks could be seen and heard for miles.[15]

The restaurant is truly the center of Gary Peele's life. His father is the manager; his mother does the books; and he is the all-around busboy/decorator/errand runner. He also becomes a keeper of secrets when he discovers that Dunlinger's daughter is in love with the handicapped school teacher who in the evenings plays the piano. Although Kerr probably added the love story to hold her readers' attention, the story she really wants them to understand is the one about bigotry and prejudice.

While Mr. Dunlinger proudly proclaims that he does not like "bigotry of any sort!" he nevertheless instructs waiters to seat attractive people by the windows where they can be seen and unattractive ones and those with children in the back near The Grill. Even though Gary tells the story, occasional chapters are interspersed with the letters and the journal that his brother, Bobby, writes as he endures the war in Saudi Arabia. Despite their quarrel, Mr. Dunlinger puts Bobby's picture up at the restaurant and makes everyone feel good about Berryville having its own soldier in the Gulf.

Gradually, readers learn that Bobby's quarrel with Mr. Dunlinger had been over Bobby's direct, and Mr. Dunlinger's indirect, part in forcing a struggling little Mexican restaurant out of business through a combination of hostile, ethnic-based rumors and the instigation of raids by immigration officials to check for undocumented workers. When the Mexican family's son commits suicide and Bobby recognizes that he has played a role in something truly evil, he quarrels with Mr. Dunlinger and swears he will never again set foot in the Linger Restaurant.

Near the end of the war—actually after the treaty has been signed—Bobby is wounded; one of his best friends is killed and another one horribly wounded. Bobby's homecoming is delayed by several weeks while Bobby is treated in a hospital. This gives Mr. Dunlinger time to drum up a huge welcome-home party scheduled for the Fourth of July. Bobby, who now has to wear a hearing aid and walk with a cane, reluctantly agrees to participate. The grand plans fall apart, however, when Bobby's terribly disfigured friend shows up for the event and Mr. Dunlinger asks Bobby to send him away because "how could we expect people to enjoy their lunch, looking at . . . that poor fella—his face isn't even human anymore. . . ." (*Linger*, 203)

Bobby and his friend and their girlfriends, along with Gary and his girlfriend, Sloan, leave Mr. Linger's party and spend the afternoon telephoning newspapers and radio stations. "Mr. Dunlinger had a lot of coverage in the weeks to come, not quite the kind he'd planned" (*Linger*, 106). For a while, the restaurant is blackballed by most of its best customers, but by the time "they televised the Clarence Thomas nomination hearings for the Supreme Court, the bar and The Grill were jammed with after-dinner drinkers hanging around to watch Anita Hill. . . ." (*Linger*, 210). Gary's girlfriend, Sloan, who all along had been collecting news clippings and asking questions about "the yellow ribbon war," names her collection "Playing Gulf" and submits it at school for her Current Events project. She "got a B minus, with a note reading 'Provocative but dated, don't you think? We're Current Events, not History.' The 'current' was underlined" (*Linger*, 211).

This closing incident was probably Kerr speaking through her character in hopes that she could keep *Linger* from suffering the same fate as Sloan's paper.

Shoebag and *Shoebag Returns*

In 1990, M. E. Kerr launched a new career for herself as a writer of books for children rather than for teenagers. She had a new publisher, Scholastic, and a new name for herself, Mary James.

Shoebag got a starred review in *School Library Journal,*[16] where Patricia Manning called it "a nifty twist on Kafka, a la *Metamorphosis.*" Other reviewers praised its originality, the clever details, and the fast moving plot. The title character is a cockroach who turns into a boy. He is named from his place of birth but as a boy takes the name of Stuart Bagg. At first his metamorphosis just happens, but then he learns from Gregor Samsa, a predecessor who decides to remain in human form, how to control the change so he can go back and forth and enjoy both worlds.

Roaches have been around for 250 million years; in fact, they were here 249 million years before people were. Kerr makes their ability to survive all the more intriguing by placing them in contemporary settings where they plan their lives around the schedules of exterminators and their moves from one home to another around the mailing of parcels in which they hitch rides.

The morning after Shoebag finds himself in the body of a small boy, he is afraid to go to school and begs his mother, who is still a cockroach, to come with him. As she climbs into his pencil box, he promises her that "It's all right if you nap, just as long as I know you're with me, that's what counts." She is with him all right— even at lunch when a squeamish little girl sees her and screeches not once, but twice, "YEEEEEEEEEEEEOWWWWWWW! A COCK-ROACH!"[17]

Thank goodness for the mysterious Gregor Samsa, who restores order while saving the life of Shoebag's mother. Samsa also appears in the sequel, where Stuart finds himself in Miss Rattray's School for Girls "and now one boy." The "one boy" is such a pitiful case that Shoebag promises to be his pal and so transforms himself back into Stuart Bagg.

The Shuteyes

The second of the Mary James books for middle grade readers, *The Shuteyes* is a humorous reversal of the parental advice of "Get to bed now" and "You need your sleep." Most of the action takes place on the planet Alert, which, according to the inhabitants' myths, was created in six days because "the Lord didn't rest." On Alert it is a crime to sleep, and no one says five-letter words in polite company. Instead, they spell them out: S-l-e-e-p, t-i-r-e-d, w-e-a-r-y, s-l-a-c-k, d-r-e-a-m, s-n-o-r-e.

The people do not even have television because viewers might be tempted to watch in a supine position and doze off. Those who insist on sleeping are considered freaks and are banished to institutions or exiled to South Alert. Upstanding citizens fear that the condition might be catching, as shown in this conversation between Chester and Angel, which is a wonderful example of interactive literature. Try reading the following lines without yawning.

> "You think if you hang around with Cyril you'll close your eyes or something like that?"
> "Yes. Close my eyes, and maybe even yawn."
> *Yawn.*
> Why did she have to say that word.
> Who can hear the word "yawn," and not yawn?
> In Alert the word "yawn" didn't make people yawn, but I was forced to turn away from Angel, and pretend to look for Mr. Quick at the top of The Star Reacher. I yawnnnnned, quietly as I could, sure she might even hear my jaws move it was such a long, luxurious yawn.[18]

The Shuteyes was not as well received as was *Shoebag,* partly because few readers in the target audience of grades 4 through 7 (the protagonist is 11 years old) are sophisticated enough to understand satire. Also, as Ruth Vose said when she reviewed the book in *School Library Journal,* "Keeping up with all the characters and twists of plot requires close attention. *The Shuteyes,* in its own way is a multilayered experience: a humorous, slightly scary adventure; a cautionary tale; and an exploration of the absurdity of prejudice, all rolled into one."[19]

Kerr said she was not as surprised at children missing the point as she was at the adults who thought the book was about sleep deprivation. She wanted to write a book about prejudice that would show how it develops and grows, so she tried to think of something that everybody does. Besides going to the bathroom—which obviously would not have been an appropriate topic—sleep was the only thing she could think of. She never dreamed people would interpret it literally.

Frankenlouse

By October of 1994 when *Frankenlouse*, the third Mary James book, was published, Kerr was feeling confident enough about writing for fifth and sixth graders that, on the cover, Mary James is identified as "also known as M. E. Kerr."

Nick, the 14-year-old protagonist, introduces himself by telling how the year before, when his parents were still together, the three of them had gone on a camping trip. He relates that as he was sitting on a dock with a fishing pole but really thinking about drawing a cartoon featuring a gentleman carrying a pair of hands into a hand laundry, his father shouts, "Nick! Don't move!"

After his father kicks away a poisonous snake that had been poised to strike, Nick says "It would never have occurred to me to disobey an order. I am a child of discipline . . . and I would have been dead if I had not been Patch Reber's son."[20]

Patch Reber is not only Nick's father, he is also a West Point graduate, a Vietnam veteran, "a control freak," and commanding officer of Blister Military Academy where Nick is a student.

Although the school is not treated nearly so seriously, it is nevertheless a boy's version of the private school in *Is That You, Miss Blue?* The school is going coed; there are five girls compared to the 150 boys, and, as with several of Kerr's stories, one of the girls is the daughter of a celebrity of dubious fame. As in *What I Really Think of You* and *I'll Love You When You're More Like Me*, a major conflict in the story is the pressure that fathers put on their sons to follow in the father's career. Nick's father wants him to graduate from Blister Military Academy and go on to become a third-generation West Pointer. Nick's mother is much more sympathetic with his desire to become a cartoonist and suggests that he come and live with her in New York and apply for admission at the High School of Music and Art. In a good compromise, Nick splits the difference by deciding to stay at the military academy until he graduates. But instead of living in the relative luxury of his father's house, he is going to move into the dorms with the other boys, and instead of applying to West Point for college, he will apply to art school.

At 14, Nick is almost as old as some of the characters in Kerr's young adult novels, and he faces the same kinds of problems. When asked why she considers *Frankenlouse* a children's book and *Dinky Hocker* a young adult book, Kerr said that the main difference is that she forced herself to drastically reduce the number of subplots. With *Frankenlouse*, her editor, Ann Wright, encouraged her to cut back even further. Kerr sounded almost wistful as she mused that Nick's cartoon strip used to have "a lot more life to it." Kerr also wrote shorter sentences and shorter paragraphs and organized them into shorter chapters; some consisting of only two or three pages. The tone is also lighter.

Even in her books for more mature readers, Kerr says she is now telling her stories with fewer characters and working to keep the plots moving in one direction. In the 25 years she has been writing for teenagers, she has seen a shortening of attention spans. Today's kids will not work as hard to get a story, probably because they have so many other entertainment options: music, videos, computers, after-school activities, part-time jobs, or just hanging around with friends. Ironically, at the same time this is happening, many publishers have changed from identifying their young adult books as "ages 12-up" to "ages 10-up."

5. Her Humor

Oh, of course, the past improves. Believe me, I would never have written a book like that at the time. I was brooding, I was always in trouble, and while those jokes and things that I used to play on people in school seem funny now, at the time they weren't funny.

from M. E. Kerr talking about the humor in
ME ME ME ME ME (Sutton, 27)

Whereas almost any fiction writer is pleased about making readers smile or laugh, Kerr is unusual in that she not only creates humor, she thinks about it and has her characters talk about it. In a *School Library Journal* interview, she spoke about how she could never use in her books some of the humorous but insulting jibes that she heard from a group of kids she was working with. One white girl talked about whether she had dressed "too black today," while others joked about how they would not be seen in public with the black boys but how they would kiss them because they have "the best lips." A black girl teased a Costa Rican girl by calling her "yellow-face," to which the Costa Rican responded "I'd bite you, but I'd get AIDS." Kerr was amazed. She said,

> They're little twelve-year-olds, doing these jigsaw puzzles right out of school and they talked that way to each other all through this session. They didn't know each other at all. Nobody got mad, nobody started a fight; it's just the way they talk. . . . [H]umor, of course, is a great weapon. A lot of what they said to each other was humorous. (Sutton, 28)

Kerr concluded that the joking was probably "a natural process of absorbing each other's differences." And although today's ideas of multiculturalism and political correctness will keep Kerr from using examples like the ones she observed, she nevertheless uses humor to explore differences.

Little Little was Kerr's most difficult book to write because she wanted it to be funny. She said that "when you're writing about handicapped people it's hard for you as an outsider to have the insider humor without being either patronizing or cruel. Finding the right voice is hard." She could not get Roach to sound natural, and Little Little "sounded self-pitying or sad or melancholy." Kerr wanted Little Little to come across as a strong character, a survivor, someone that readers would feel was going to be okay. Only when Kerr realized that "it could have happened to me," did she find a voice:

> a sassy voice—a voice very similar to my own when I was a kid. . . . I was that smartmouth. I would have been angry. I would have found the humor in it. I would have liked the ones who weren't perfectly formed, and I wouldn't have liked my mother's suggestions at finding the ones who were. (Roginsky, 38)

The voice that Kerr found for her protagonist shows up in this protest from an exasperated Little Little after her mother criticizes Sydney Cinnamon yet again:

> If Pablo Picasso had a wart on his finger, he wouldn't be the world-famous painter in your eyes, he'd be that fellow with the wart on his finger who paints! You are all caught up in and bogged down in p.f.! Sydney Cinnamon has one of the best minds of anyone who's ever sat down at our dinner table and all you see is the tooth that sticks out! (*Little,* 179–80)

The relationship between Little Little and her mother sounds much like the one between Marijane and Mrs. Meaker. The two had a running argument about wit and humor as described in *ME ME ME ME ME:*

> "I'm telling you this for your own good. Boys don't like girls who cut up."
> "I'm not living my life for what boys like."

"They don't like girls who crack jokes all the time and are
bent on being comedians."

"Who cares? Who cares? Who cares?"

"You're going to care, pull-lenty, when all the other girls get
boyfriends and you don't. You'll be the comedian, hah? There
isn't a female comedian alive who's happy. . . . Oh, they get up
onstage and get laughs and make fools out of themselves, let
their faces and bodies get into all sorts of ungraceful positions,
but when the curtain comes down, it's another story." (*ME,* 72)

In *The Son of Someone Famous,* Kerr has Adam Blessing go
home after meeting Brenda Belle in the drugstore and write a line
in his journal, "I like funny girls. I always have."[1] Adam's reason
is that funny girls are so much easier to talk to. Regardless of
whether Adam's opinion is typical of real-life boys, the line in the
story is wish-fulfilling both for Kerr and for the bright and witty
girls who are attracted to her books.

A variation on this theme appears in her science fiction *The
Shuteyes,* in which Lornge is punished because he persists in loving Tweetie, a parrot who cannot help going to sleep. One of the
reasons he has "the stick-by-me's" for Tweetie is that she knows
more "you-tell-'ems" than anyone:

> "You tell 'em, Goldfish. You've been around the globe."
> "You tell 'em, Pieface. You've got the crust."
> "You tell 'em, Parcel Post. I can't express it." (*Shuteyes,* 155)

Because *Night Kites* is such a somber story, Kerr may have
worked harder to include humor. One of her techniques was to
have the characters talk about humor. Fairly early in the story,
Peter and Erick figure out that their Dad tries to cover his ner-
vousness by telling strings of jokes that are not very funny. Like
bad puns, they are trite and interrupt the flow of conversation,
but they help their father get through tough situations.

As much as Erick dislikes his dad's habit, he himself does something similar but with smart aleck remarks that make his Dad
shout "I won't take his mouth!" When Erick's mother tries to
defend him by saying, "You never understood survival humor,

never, Arthur!" the dad pouts, "Another of my failings! . . . I'll add it to the list. . . ." (*Kites*, 185). But not even Erick's best friend likes his jokes. Jack complains, "You've got a million zingers, but not one word of advice" (*Kites*, 103). Nicki is more appreciative. When she gets out of the car for the Senior Ball wearing stockings and a hair ribbon with dalmatian spots on them, Roman Knight calls out from between a row of cars "Nicki? Woof woof!"

"What am I going to do about him?" she asks Erick, who responds "Bark back?" She laughs and says:

> "I love you because you're funny. I like funny. Jack was never
> funny. Even Ski was never funny. Am I funny?"
> "You're funny. But not ha ha funny."
> "Do you love me anyway?"
> "I love you, Nicki, but you're not easy."
> "You had easy," she said, "and it bored you. . . ." (*Kites*, 191)

Kerr says that she wants to woo young readers "not just with entertaining stories, but also with subject matter which will provoke concern and a questioning about this complicated and often unfair world we live in." Although she wants her readers to laugh, she also wants them to "be introspective . . . and I hope I can give them characters and situations which will inspire these reactions."[2]

One of the ways she does this is to illustrate how a culture's attitudes and beliefs are reflected in its jokes. In *Night Kites*, after Peter has been hospitalized and Erick's dad comes to tell him the bad news, the first thing Erick thinks about are the jokes he has heard about AIDS:

> Q: What do the letters GAY stand for?
> A: Got AIDS yet?
> Q: Did you hear about the new disease gay musicians are com-
>   ing down with?
> A: BAND-AIDS
> Q: What do you call a faggot in a wheelchair?
> A: ROLLAIDS (*Kites*, 88)

When Pete comes home from the hospital, he and Erick have their first conversation. The tone is lightened by Pete's reference to a Gay Writer's Discussion Group and their dad's question "Is a gay book a book that sleeps with other books of the same sex?" Pete starts his explanation with:

> Well, Ricky, this is sort of a variation on that joke about the gay guy trying to convince his mother he's really a drug addict. You've probably heard it. (*Kites,* 90)

Eventually Pete must tell the family that he is gay and has AIDS. A foreshadowing of the trauma this will precipitate comes during a scene in which Charlie Gilhooley has both of his arms broken when he is thrown out of the bar that Nicki's father owns. Erick's friend says that, after Toledo belted Charlie, he picked him up and threw him out the door. Then, when Toledo started to walk away, Charlie managed to prop himself up on one elbow and call out to Toledo, "Yoo hoo, I forgive you."

> "That's a crappy joke," I said.
> "It didn't happen that way at all," said Nicki. "See, once they start coming into a place, then others follow, that's what Daddy says, so Toledo asked him to leave before he even served him. But Charlie wouldn't."
> "I'm just trying to make a joke of it," Jack said, "You know: What do you call a gay bar without bar stools? A fruit stand." (*Kites,* 59)

Kerr steers away from this tense conversation by having Erick's girlfriend, Dill, ask him "Honey? Do you think you'll ever laugh at anything again?" He scores a point in their running argument by whispering back, "Sweetheart? When you don't ever have sex, your muscles freeze in one position, making it impossible to laugh" (*Kites,* 59).

Kerr's understanding of the small differences that can change the tone of a joke is illustrated by Erick's musing about why most of the jokes he has heard have not been about "gay guys"; "They were always about 'fags,' 'fruits,' worse." Another example of the

In 1990 Alison Gray interviewed Kerr for an article in *VOYA (Voice of Youth Advocates).*

subtlety in Kerr's humor surfaces in *Night Kites,* in which she contrives a planet where there are no smells except for a delicious, wonderful perfume that fills the air before someone dies. In the somber ending to the tale, Peter reads to Erick the beginning of a short story he has written, entitled "The Sweet Perfume of Good-Bye."

The next year, Kerr used the title and the same metaphor for a wryly humorous, or at least ironic, short story published in *Visions: Nineteen Short Stories by Outstanding Writers for Young Adults.* Changing the tone from sad to funny, she has Caroline, the 17-year-old narrator, introduce herself by explaining that she has a sense of humor. Caroline has been sent alone on a fact-finding mission to another planet where there are no smells except in the hour (this revised time limit is crucial to the new story) before death, when the dying person gives off an intoxicatingly beautiful and haunting scent. In the first few sentences Caroline explains that "The fresh-cut bright green grass where my lovers sit does not even smell. . . ." Then she interrupts herself with:

> I call them "my lovers" with a little smile. That is my sense of humor emerging (though I am thought to be a humorless young scientist). They do not make love to me, of course. They are mine only in the fact that I am studying them.[3]

The plan is for Caroline to be picked up after she has finished her observations. When Doctor Orr signals her that he has arrived with the rocket to return her to earth, she has mixed emotions. Just after she tells him that she will need about an hour and 15 minutes to get herself to the landing field, he radios:

> "My God, Caroline, I'm almost overwhelmed by this wonderful fragrance here!"
> "A fragrance, Doctor Orr? Not on Farfire. You see—"
> He interrupts me with a whoop of joy. "*Un*believable. Almost like lilies! It's come upon me suddenly! Caroline? It's so all pervasive! It's on *me!* My hands, my face—it's the sweetest perfume!"
> Of course, I cannot get to him in time.
> I sit down right where I am and make my entry.
> I write *I think I've lost my ride home.*
> In the interest of accuracy, I cross out "I think." (*Perfume,* 190)

In another science fiction setting, on the Planet Alert in *The Shuteyes*, Kerr teaches readers about using humor as a trial balloon or as a shield to hide behind. Chester's mother tells him how to get out of his hypnotically induced fogs. He is to say:

> "If you mess with my head, you'll be better off dead." Then you say, "only kidding."
> "Why say only kidding?"
> "To be on the safe side. You always want to be on the safe side when you make a threat."
> "Then what good is the threat?
> "Threats are good to give you time to run." (*Shuteyes,* 15)

Kerr illustrates the use of humor as a different kind of defense in *Is That You, Miss Blue?* Flanders goes into the bathroom that she and Agnes have been assigned to share with Miss Blue and finds hanging on the wall a "crown-of-thorn-type" picture of Jesus with the verse:

> O bleeding face, O face divine,
> Be love and adoration thine.

If someone her own age had been with Flanders, the two would have collapsed on the floor in a giggling fit—"not that the idea of Christ's bleeding face was funny, but things out of context often seem preposterous." Because Flanders is facing this alone, except for Miss Blue waiting for a comment, her reaction is one of self-consciousness. She resents the fact that Miss Blue has been foisted off on her, and she knows that to contend with the situation she will "make it all a joke, one big laugh to share with everyone" (*Blue,* 27).

The eternal conflict between young and old is grist for many a writer's humor mill. Those who write for young people view parent-child disagreements from the perspective of the young, who make fun of parents and other authority figures. In *Night Kites*, Pete teases his uptight father by telling him that his fellow teachers drink "because they all regret not choosing business careers where they can make upward of sixty and seventy thousand a year" (*Kites,* 30). Pete and Erick defend themselves from their father's lectures by labeling them: Rap #1 "The Family Is First," Rap #2 "Pull Yourself Up by Your Own Bootstraps," which is a twin to Rap #3 "Learn the Value of a Dollar" (*Kites,* 40).

In *I'll Love You When You're More Like Me*, Wally refers to his boss at the soda shop as a "wrap-around baldie" (*Like Me,* 25). In *Linger*, when the Peele family goes into New York for their annual Christmas outing with obnoxious Uncle Chad, the lawyer who thinks he is smarter than his restaurant-manager brother, Gary nostalgically wishes that Bobby were with them so he could tell one of the put-down jokes he saves for just such occasions:

Uncle Chad, why did the elephant in the forest stop to eat a huge pile of lion dung? . . . You give up? Because he'd just swallowed a lawyer, and he wanted to get the bad taste out of his mouth. (*Linger*, 48)

In *The Son of Someone Famous*, Brenda Belle Blossom goes bird watching with Milton Merrensky, who is not the typical teenage hero. When Brenda Belle's mother sighs, "I wouldn't be interested in him for a boyfriend," Brenda Belle answers, "He wouldn't be interested in you for a girlfriend either" (*Famous*, 226).

This is more than a ploy on Kerr's part to give vicarious pleasure to kids who would not or could not say such a thing to their own mothers. It is an indication of Brenda Belle's newly earned independence of thought and the fact that she is beginning to see past the sequestered little world of teenage values in Storm, Vermont.

At least with Kerr, her young protagonists are just as critical of people their own age as they are of adults, and she lets the grownups have some of the good lines, too. In "Sunny Days and Sunny Nights," published in *Connections: Short Stories by Outstanding Writers for Young Adults*,[5] Marybeth is going with a boy who announces at dinner that "Females prefer chunky peanut butter over smooth forty-three percent to thirty-nine percent, while men show an equal liking for both." He plans to go into marketing and "prides himself on knowing what sells, and why, and what motivates people" (*Sunny*, 218). When they kiss, Marybeth suspects that he is thinking about what percentage of females as compared to males close their eyes while smooching. She had temporarily broken up with Sunny, her true love, who joined the Navy. Her father snidely remarks that the Navy will make a man out of him. When Marybeth argues that he is already a man, her father shakes his head and says, "You only have to listen to all that talk about the big waves, the surf, the beach—either he's a boy or a fish. . . ." (*Sunny*, 219).

In developing characterization, Kerr makes humor play a double role. When a character explains a serious point through an amusing comparison, readers get the idea, plus they learn a bit more about how the character thinks. In *What I Really Think of You*, Opal Ringer prepares readers to understand her brother's frustration by observing that he was "supposed to be following in Daddy's footsteps, but it was like an ant trying to put his legs down in elephant tracks." His sermons "got worse as he went along. His nerve ran out on him, like a cat running from the fleas on her own back" (*Think*, 7).

In *Is That You, Miss Blue?* Cardmaker's description of "The Rich" in such places as "their drawing room," "their Rolls Royce," "on their way to the stock market," and "just coming back from safari" reveals more about Cardmaker's lack of experience than it does about "The Rich."

In *Him She Loves?* Henry's brothers spot his love symptoms and advise against "getting a thing" on Valerie. Henry protests, "Why do you make it sound like I'm growing a wart, or getting a fungus between my toes? I suppose you and Fred fall in love, but I get a thing."

"It's the way you go about it," Ernie answers. "You throw yourself at it like someone jumping into a fireman's net from a burning building." In spite of his brother's warnings, Henry goes right ahead and throws himself into trying to make Valerie love him as he loves her (*Him*, 42).

Kerr surprises readers by digging out life's incongruities and sprinkling them throughout her writing. In *Linger*, Bobby Peele writes in his journal about spending Christmas in Saudi Arabia:

> Free everything courtesy of corporate America. Suntan lotion from Avon, disposable cameras from Kodak, golf balls from Wilson, and just in case the Iraqis don't kill us, Phillip Morris sends cigarettes to do it. (*Linger*, 31)

In *I'll Love You When You're More Like Me*, Kerr slips in another antismoking message. When Wally first meets Sabra St. Amour on the beach, she asks him for a cigarette. Wally responds "You'd have to be a little crazy to let the tobacco companies manipulate you. . . . Why do you think they'd name a cigarette something like Merit? Merit's supposed to mean excellence, value, reward. What's so excellent, valuable and rewarding about having cancer?" Sabra's flip reply is that she has heard of coming to the beach for a suntan, a swim, or a walk, but never for a lecture. Wally is undaunted, realizing that he has stumbled onto an idea that is not half bad. He continues with "Vantage—as in advantage; True; More; Now . . . Live for the moment because you won't live long. Get More. Be True to your filthy habit" (*Like Me*, 24–25).

In *If I Love You, Am I Trapped Forever?* readers smile at the incongruous images that Alan evokes when he says that, whenever Catherine Stein mentions her son, it is "like the Mona Lisa suddenly looking down from her frame and launching into a discussion of the local Chevrolet dealer, the Avon lady, or the bow-legged boy who lived across the street" (*Trapped,* 22).

The incongruity of mixing humor and religion is a recurring element in *Is That You, Miss Blue?* When Mr. Dibblee, a newly rich father, comes to take his daughter and her friends out to dinner, he tells a joke about an Episcopalian minister who was often mistaken for a Catholic priest. The punch line is "He's no Father, he's got four kids!" (*Blue,* 83) Headmistress Anna P. Ettinger pretends not to hear a word that Mr. Dibblee says in answer to her explanation that Cardmaker cannot leave the campus because she is being disciplined.

> Well, who among us don't have sin, as the Bible says? Some of the greatest saints were sinners, ma'am. Moses murdered an Egyptian and hid him in the sand; David was an adulterer who took away the wives of three men; Jacob was a liar and a thief, deceived his blind and aging papa so he could get something didn't belong to him . . . and old Mary Magdalene was a hooker. (*Blue,* 80)

Mr. Dibblee's daughter is so embarrassed that she turns pale, whereas Flanders has to "concentrate on national disasters to keep from laughing" (*Blue,* 80).

Kerr's short story "Do You Want My Opinion,"[5] published in *Sixteen: Short Stories by Outstanding Writers for Young Adults,* is based on a reversal of expectations. It begins with a boy worrying about the dreams he has and lamenting that he is tired of putting his head under the cold-water faucet. He dreamed that Cynthia Slater asked his opinion about *The Catcher in the Rye* and that he told Lauren Lake what he thought about John Lennon's music, Picasso's art, and Russian/American relations.

Readers soon catch on that, in this story, people freely touch, hug, fondle, and kiss each other but scrupulously avoid talking about anything important. After all, although bodies are all alike, ideas are individual and personal. Getting so intimate with someone that you talk about the books they have read or ask what they think about World War II is "a good way to cheapen the exchange of ideas" (*Opinion,* 96), Of course this reversal provides for some amusing images as when the school graffiti artists draw heads identified with the initials of suspected thinkers, and in the boys' bathroom they write such messages as "If you'd like some interesting conversation, try Loulou" (*Opinion,* 95).

A variation on this theme brings a quiet smile in *Dinky Hocker Shoots Smack!* when Tucker expects to be chewed out by P. John "for suckering him into a date" with overweight Dinky, but all P. John says is "Susan's got a mind like a steel trap. She's okay!" Tucker is surprised because he "had never given any thought to Dinky's mind. It was not the main thing the average person meeting Dinky noticed" (*Dinky,* 55).

For pure hilarity, few scenes rival Kerr's description of the evening that P. John and Tucker take Dinky and Natalia to a dance. The scene begins with P. John's arrival at Tucker's house, where everyone is preparing for the opening of Mr. Woolf's new Help Yourself health food store. P. John nods his head "in that old wiser-than-all-the-world way" and says "You'll probably attract a lot of radicals." He goes on to explain that radicals are often health nuts and vegetarians. As examples he cites Hitler and George Bernard Shaw, hastening to explain that Hitler was an exception because most such people "are weak-sister socialists like Shaw." When the amazed Mr. Tucker says, "I suppose you prefer Hitler," P. John says that he does not agree with Hitler all down the line, but at least "he didn't cozy up to the Communists like a lot of jelly-spined liberals" (*Dinky,* 48–49).

At Dinky's house, P. John makes an equally startling impression on Dinky's parents. When Mr. Hocker hands over money for taxi fare because he feels the subway is unsafe for coming home after the dance, P. John hands it back, maintaining that he is one of the few New Yorkers not on the dole. When Mr. Hocker wants to check watches as he instructs the boys to get the girls home by 12, P. John says "I don't own a watch anymore. A mugger relieved me of it in September, no doubt so he could report to the unemployment office in time to sign for his check" (*Dinky,* 49–50).

The evening goes on in much the same vein. By the end, Tucker is perspiring "worse than a Rose Bowl tackle on New Year's Eve" (*Dinky,* 54). He has also decided that he is boring, a failure on the dating scene, obnoxious and bumptious, and just generally socially inadequate. That the beautiful Natalia still likes him is enough to warm the hearts of insecure readers everywhere. One of the strengths of Kerr's books is that she shows readers that there is room for the less-than-perfect, for those who are not blessed with the unlimited self-confidence that pours out from most mass media presentations of the great American dream.

After the awards ceremony, a very upset Mrs. Hocker and a very angry Mr. Hocker are looking for Dinky because of her graffiti message "Dinky Hocker shoots smack!" Tucker feels sorry for Natalia, who has to stay home and hide Dinky as well as fend off Mrs. Hocker's rage. But then Mr. Hocker says to Tucker: "You come along to the deli with me" (*Dinky,* 185), and suddenly Tucker feels sorry for himself. Readers who have been in similar situations smile with understanding at Tucker's predicament.

A sudden realization that other people's minds work the same as one's own is not likely to make readers laugh, but it will make them grin as when—in *Fell*—John tells Delia that he loves her, and she responds:

> "Don't make me say I love you, Fell."
> "Who said you had to say it?"
> "I thought you'd expect it because you said it."

"I did, but I'm not going to stay awake nights if you don't say
it." I stayed awake a lot of nights because she didn't say it. I
knew I would when I said I wasn't going to stay awake nights if
she didn't say it. (*Fell*, 128)

Both teenagers and adults are interested in the bizarre, the
weird, and the grotesque; witness the popularity of tabloid newspapers, TV talk shows, and urban legends. Kerr was ahead of her
time when she had Dinky share such stories as the one about the
man with the wooden arm who would bang on the windshields of
young lovers' cars and try to get in to steal the girls away. Dinky
swears that a girl who went to St. Marie's had been up in
Prospect Park with her boyfriend. They started talking about the
man and grew so frightened that they drove away. The boy took
the girl home and then went to his own house. When he opened
his door, he found a hook from a wooden arm caught in the door
handle.

In *Frankenlouse*, humor is at a junior high level when Nick
describes faculty member Captain Tuttle as a "world class nose
picker, an officer whose morning breath lasted all day long." At
the end of the year, "when the yearbook featured everyone's 'faculty buddy,' no one wanted Tuttle," so Nick's dad makes him do
the honors. But as Nick explains, "This sacrifice on my part did
nothing to endear me to him. Tuttle was not won over easily. People who smell like Tuttle are strangers to kindness. It makes
them suspicious" (*Frankenlouse*, 30).

For older readers, Kerr's references to death may bring either
shudders or smiles. In *Is That You, Miss Blue?* Sumner Thomas,
Flanders's blind date, is preoccupied with suicide because his
mother, a very dramatic person, committed suicide on Christmas
Eve and left a note saying "Everyone is to blame for this. Everyone who reads this note or hears about it" (*Blue*, 70). During all
the slow dances, Sumner tells Flanders the intriguing details that
he intends to put in a book called "Killing Yourself Successfully."
As Sumner explains, it is not as easy as it seems. Artist Arshile
Gorky "hung nooses all over his Connecticut property until he got
the nerve to put his head through one." A psychologist named

Stekel killed himself by swallowing 22 bottles of aspirin after he had made a study of suicide. Sumner thinks that if he himself were to commit suicide, he would jump because "it's still a very sure way" (*Blue,* 109), even though someone who does it is admitting that he thinks he has fallen from favor.

In *I'll Love You When You're More Like Me,* Wally's biggest problem is that he is his mortician father's only son and thus is expected to take over the family business. Wally hates the idea, especially the succession part, which makes his father's profession sound "like vampirism which has to be passed on to each succeeding generation" (*Like Me,* 44). All his life he has been teased with crude jokes about "just dying to see you" and with singing telephone calls: "The worms crawl in, the worms crawl out." Wally consoled himself with the idea that these erstwhile friends would sooner or later be wheeled to the Witherspoon mortuary, but even that failed to comfort him when he remembered he was in line to be the next embalmer. His mother's advice was to answer crank calls with "You are an ill person and you should see a doctor." Wally's little sister says exactly this, and when her mother smiles approvingly, she adds as a kicker, "And after you die from your illness, we'll be seeing you!"

Wally writes an A+ essay on "Fear and Funerals," in which he points out that people do not wear black out of respect for the dead but instead to be inconspicuous so that the ghost of the corpse will not notice them near the coffin and try to lure them to their deaths, too. Coffins are carried out of the church feet first to keep the corpse from looking back and beckoning one of the family to follow. Long, exaggerated eulogies and flowers are given to appease the ghost, whereas the music and a handful of dirt tossed into the open grave are to lay its spirit to rest.

Wally's mortician father, on a scale of one to ten, ranks as a minus one when it comes to curiosity about funeral superstitions. Wally assumes that it is because "he still carries with him a lot of the old guilt undertakers used to have about the profession" (*Like Me,* 121). Many of them would live in towns miles away from their mortuaries and commute to work as if they were shopkeepers or salesmen.

Kerr makes life in the mortuary believable with homey details such as that an open coffin is a tempting napping place for the family cat and that what is served for dinner depends on whether there is "a guest." People do not want to smell corned beef and cabbage when they come to pay their last respects.

Kerr uses less-than-lovable insects as another way to flirt with the grotesque. Her title *Frankenlouse* hardly inspires warm and fuzzy feelings, and, as one of her characters might put it, she "has a thing about cockroaches." When asked if this came from a love of Franz Kafka's "The Metamorphosis" or from living for 10 years in a New York City apartment, she was quick to say she has no love for cockroaches. She hates them! When writing about them, she is playing a mind game to see what it is like to take a point of view contrary to her real feelings.

Sydney, her dwarf hero in *Little Little*, is nicknamed Roach because he wears a cockroach costume and does commercials and public appearances for an exterminator company. The irony is that, when courting Little Little, the deformed Roach wins out over his competitor, who is outwardly perfect but inwardly crooked. One of the funniest scenes in *Little Little* occurs when Sydney is called into the principal's office and is scolded for singing his theme song, "La Cucaracha," in a school assembly.

> "You're some kind of a smart aleck, aren't you, Cinnamon?"
> "What do you mean, sir?"
> "Singing about marihuana that way."
> "That's the song," I said. "I didn't make up the words."
> "You didn't make up porque la falta, marihuana que fumar?"
> "That's the song," I said. "La cucaracha, la cucaracha doesn't want to travel on because she hasn't marihuana for to smoke."
> (*Little*, 99)

In spite of the explanation, Sydney suspects that the principal does not believe him because he thinks marihuana is some new weed discovered in the seventies.

In both *Shoebag* books about the cockroach who mysteriously changes into a boy, there are lots of details to make readers smile. Even in the semiserious scene when Stuart is trying to decide whether to return from his cockroach form to his human form, the overriding tone is one of humor.

> "How would *they* like it," Under the Toaster used to say of humans, "if someday creatures a hundred times their size gassed them—pfft—like they were mindless, heartless, unfeeling flecks of flesh, put on earth only to annoy them?" . . . Why would he want to become the very enemy who had uprooted his family's home, invented a noxious substance like Zap (which had nearly killed him) and through the years stepped on his kind, designed lethal roach motels for his kind, and always looked upon any critter from roachdom with loathing.
>
> Still, one thing cockroaches were known for was loyalty. Gas them, they would return. Smoke them out, they would be back. Tear down their buildings, they would remain in the neighborhood.[6]

With such thoughts as this, Shoebag, "frail and shaken from everything that had happened to him," returned to "the Changing Room," where students change into their athletic clothes but where Shoebag transforms himself from a roach into a human.

In summary, Kerr's talent for making readers smile, if not giggle, is one of her greatest strengths. Equally important is the fact that her characters discuss humor as they show readers how many different purposes it serves. Kerr uses comedy for individual characterization as well as for exploring cultural and individual differences. Although she does not employ the terms, she introduces readers to various philosophical and psychological theories of humor including superiority, relief, conflict, and incongruity. She also utilizes jokes to illustrate cultural beliefs and prejudices and as a way for teenagers to express frustration about being under the thumb of adults. And perhaps most important of all, her wit shines a light on life's enigmas and unfairnesses. When seen through a smile, these puzzles do not seen nearly so daunting.

6. Her Names

They always seem to have names like that, don't they? Rich, beautiful girls are never named Elsie Pip or Mary Smith.

from Gentlehands

When asked about the energy she devotes to creating names for characters, places, and even things, Kerr said that as long as she can remember she has had an interest in names. The credit goes to Charles Dickens and to her father, who, when he was reading to her, would pick out some character and say, "Now what if that man had been called Mr. Smith?" In Kerr's forthcoming book on creative writing, she plans to ask young readers something similar: "What if Holden Caulfield had been called Jim Jackson?"

In several of her books, Kerr acknowledges the debt she owes Charles Dickens by making direct references to some of his names. Both in *Is That You, Miss Blue?* and in *ME ME ME ME ME*, she identifies the names of dormitories at her school as having been drawn from Charles Dickens novels. A telephone call to Stuart Hall uncovered the fact that the school dormitories have British names—Fleet, Picadilly, High Holborn, Faith, and Upper Faith—but not from Dickens. It was Kerr's creative mind that decided to call them *Little Dorrit, David Copperfield, Hard Times*, and *Great Expectations*—all good fodder for creative punning.

In *Frankenlouse*, the students and their English teacher, Lieutenant Meadow, search for interesting names in *Hard Times*:

Mrs. Sparsit.
James Harthouse.
Tom Gradgrind.

Josiah Bounderby.

"Listen to those names! Dickens had great names for his characters!"

Someone yelled "Slackbridge!"

"Yes," Heavy Meadow [the students' name for their teacher] looked ecstatic, "Slackbridge!" (*Frankenlouse,* 83)

In Kerr's books for middle graders, astute readers could probably have guessed that Mary James was M. E. Kerr because of the way she plays with names. In general, these books offer fewer serious messages and more fun with the names.

Shoebag's title comes from the name of the leading character, a cockroach who was mysteriously changed into a person. Cockroaches, at least in the roachdom where Shoebag was born, are named for their birthplaces. His mother is named Drainboard and his father, Under the Toaster. A new baby sister is named Frying Pan, and his brothers are called Coffee Cup, Wheaties Box, and Radio. In his human form, Shoebag's name is Stuart Bagg, an especially comfortable name for young readers who probably already know and love two other literary characters who blend human and animal qualities: Bilbo Baggins from J. R. R. Tolkien's *The Hobbit* and Stuart Little from E. B. White's book of that name. In what Kerr said is a tipping of her hat to Franz Kafka, she named the boy who keeps coming to Shoebag's aid Gregor Samsa, the same name as the protagonist of Kafka's "Metamorphosis." Ten years down the road, her readers will be surprised when a second Gregor Samsa crawls into their literary consciousness.

The first clue that *The Shuteyes* is neither realistic nor oh-so-serious science fiction is the characters' names: a bird named Lornge (to rhyme with Orange); a boy named Chester Dumbello, who is of course called Dumbell; his mother, Molly Dumbello, better known as Madame Dumbello because she interprets people's dreams; his Aunt Dolly, who is called Aunt Dollar because of her wealth, and his Uncle Tux, who wears a diamond ring on every finger and a tuxedo, day or night. The Dumbellos have two neighbors. One is Gower Pye, who mysteriously disappears, and the other is Rita Box-Bender, a little white-faced, red-haired girl who is home-schooled by her widowed father. Whereas Mr. Pye's name is reminiscent of Gomer Pyle, Kerr borrowed Rita's family name from one of the upper-class British families that Evelyn Waugh wrote about in his World War II trilogy, *Men at Arms*, *Officers and Gentlemen*, and *End of the Battle*. However, there is little resemblance between that family and Rita's. The name the kids use for Rita is Worms because she has the job of sitting at a card table in front of her house under a "BAIT" sign where she sells angleworms, spot tail minnows, and dead flies. Chester's mother knows there is no money in worms and suspects that Mr. Box-Bender makes bootleg whiskey out behind the barn while Rita keeps watch at the worm stand.

All that is forgotten when Lornge takes Chester and his mother to Planet Alert; there they meet a whole new cast of interestingly named characters including Ivan Investigate, Top Security Man, Top Scientist, adoptive parents Quinten and Quinneth Quick, English teacher Lawrence Lyric, and the girl who becomes Chester's best friend, Angel Wheelspinner.

The title *Frankenlouse* capitalizes on the popularity of horror stories and the invention early in the 1990s of the word "Frankenfood" for produce that has been genetically altered to stay fresh longer. The Frankenstein connection in Kerr's title comes through a home-drawn comic strip about a book louse who lives on a library shelf in a volume of *Frankenstein*. On the same horror shelf live Spiderlouse, Dr. Jekyllouse, Tarantulalouse, and Godzillalouse. Fourteen-year-old Nick is the artist, who thinks he must have gotten his interest in drawing from his mother's side of the family since his father's relatives thought "Art was a nickname for Arthur" (*Frankenlouse*, 17). Nick attends the Blister Military Academy, whose logo was designed in such a way that most people call the school BAM. When his grandfather is feeling whimsical, he refers to West Point as Woo Poo. BAM's dorms (like the Academy and like his father and his grandfather) are named after generals, so most of the boys live in a big gray building with the gruesome name of Slaughter Hall. Nick's dad refers to Nick's friend Caleb, who always seems to be in trouble, as Collateral

Damage and to Nick's Aunt Priscilla as "Aunt Prissilly" because he blames her for Nick's mother moving to New York.

At Thanksgiving Nick goes to New York and meets his mother's new friend, Sam Saber, who, in an interesting twist on the more common practice of women writing under masculine-sounding pen names, writes nurse novels under the pseudonym of Sharon Saber: "*Nurse of the North, Nurse in Trouble, Nurse of the Arctic, Nurse of the Wilderness,* on and on" (*Frankenlouse,* 111). Kerr's awareness of ethnic fashions in names is illustrated by an African American character named Kinya Powell.

These latter examples indicate that Kerr uses names for more than just humor. She resembles a character in *Little Little* who is fittingly called Opportunity Knox because he constantly schemes to get something extra for himself. In a similar way, Kerr schemes to get extra mileage out of a limited number of words by making almost every name do double duty.

Like a poet, she manipulates sounds, relying on such devices as repetition, alliteration, and rhyme (Little Little, Belle La Belle, Carolyn Cardmaker, Wallace Witherspoon, Dirtie Dotti, Buddy Boyle, Sabra St. Amour, Gloria Gilman (nicknamed Gee Gee), $uzy $lade, and Miss Grand from Videoland). These poetic appellations serve as an amusing memory aid to readers, an important function in books that may have as many as 20 characters.

Names of people Kerr has known and been fascinated with are sprinkled throughout her books like good-luck charms. Sidney is a favorite name for boys, Belle a favorite for girls, and Blessing and Pennington are favorites for families. In *I'll Love You When You're More Like Me*, Kerr names her teenage soap opera star Sabra St. Amour after her Auburn High School French teacher. She often names a minor character after Ernest Leogrande, a man she met on the train when she was first traveling to college in Missouri. A writer who moved to New York about the same time she did, he wrote for the *New York Daily* and, until his death in 1985, was Kerr's friend and confidant. She started putting his name in her Vin Packer books and—for luck—kept the custom going with her YA books.

Kerr also creates names from sets of words that readers are accustomed to hearing together., the rock star in *I Stay Near You*, sounds familiar because he is named after Edna St. Vincent Millay, his parents' favorite poet. "Saint Vincent" is not only easy to remember but it also reminds readers of an important part of the plot. Similarly, Opal Ringer's name reminds readers that she is a have-not rather than a have, like an opal ring compared to a diamond.

In *Night Kites* Erick describes the Kingdom by the Sea motel run by Nicki's father, Captain Marr (which sounds like the French word for "sea"), as "tacky, shabby, shitty, going to rack and ruin" but at the same time bearing witness to having once "been a crazy, fantastic place: mysterious and silly and rare" (*Kites,* 140–41). The suites that face the sea have Edgar Allan Poe names: Bells, Bells, Bells; The Raven; Helen; and The Black Cat. Nicki works some afternoons at Anabel's Resale Shop, but other afternoons she and Erick swim at City By the Sea or make love in Dream Within A Dream.

The names that the characters call each other in *Night Kites* reveal their changing relationships. Nicki invents the pet name of Eri for Erick. He likes it "that she called me something as new as she was to me" (*Kites,* 165). But early on, Kerr foreshadows their breakup. When Nicki introduces Erick to her dad, he grins and says, "A new one, Fickle Pickle? Well, what's your name? . . . Rudd?" He laughingly advises, "Don't let her make your name Mud, Rudd" (*Kites,* 151).

The Rudd's family minister, Reverend Shorr, was "a thin little fellow with gold-rimmed glasses who always read his sermons and made them sound like instructions for assembling mail-order items. He was known as Reverend Snore by some of his parishioners" (*Kites,* 126). In fact, the Rudds never called him anything else, even when they were not in a humorous mood.

The special relationship between the two brothers is indicated by Peter's affectionate use of the name Ricky instead of Erick. The hostility that had long existed between Peter and his dad was illustrated by the teenage Pete calling him "O Infallible," a name that the much younger Ricky could neither understand nor pro-

For nearly 20 years, Kerr has been sharing her skill with fellow writers in a weekly workshop in East Hampton. Here she is shown with one of the members of the class.

nounce. He thought it was "O Full of Bull," the genesis of a family joke to everyone except the father (*Kites,* 159). Another bit of family history demonstrating how long Peter has known that he is gay is that at age 13 he named his dog Oscar as a secret memorial to Oscar Wilde.

A favorite way for Kerr to exhibit special relationships is to have characters create pet names for each other. In *ME ME ME ME ME,* Marijane's George calls her Agi, the Hungarian version of her middle name Agnes, whereas in *Deliver Us from Evie,* one of the early clues that Evie and Patsy Duff have a special relationship is that Evie uses the name Patty instead of Patsy because she likes "Patty better." In *Him She Loves?* Valerie's dad calls her Valley, whereas in *Linger*, Lynn complains that "Daddy's son-in-law has to be a combination of Jesus Christ, Donald Trump, and General Schwarzkopf" (*Linger,* 110), but then on a happier note she confides to Gary that Jules "calls me Ling. Nobody's ever called me by a special name. Sometimes he calls me Lingerling" (*Linger,* 111).

Less positive relationships are also depicted through names. In *If I Love You, Am I Trapped Forever?* Kerr discloses that Mrs. Stein's feelings for Alan are not nearly so strong as his feelings for her. When the two of them accidentally meet on the bus from Syracuse to Cayuta, the distraught Mrs. Stein calls him Albert instead of Alan (*Trapped,* 128). In *What I Really Think of You*, Jesse Pegler acquires further proof that he is not his father's favorite son when Reverend Pegler gives "his usual end-of-conversation benediction, 'I love you, son. I love you, Bud,' " and then corrects himself to "Jesse" (*Think,* 162).

Many times Kerr will choose a name apparently just for the sound of it, but later it crops up again in a pun. Sydney Cinnamon is a catchy, alliterative name for the dwarf hero of *Little Little*, but Kerr makes more of it than that. When Andrea Applebaum's mother hires Sydney to be Baby 1979 at a New Year's Eve party, he and Andrea grow romantic in the basement, and Andrea croons, "Cinnamon and Applebaum. Put us together and we're a pie" (*Little,* 101). Wally Witherspoon, in *If I Love You, Am I Trapped Forever?* is another alliterative name that allows Wally's "friends" to tease him about the mortuary business with such nicknames as Wither Up and Die, Withering Heights, and Wither-Away (*Trapped,* 23–25).

Early in *Little Little*, Kerr uses names not only to introduce the Twin Orphans' Home where Sydney grew up but also to amuse readers and to establish a flip, offbeat tone. Sydney, who is narrating the story, explains that he lives in Miss Lake's—commonly called Mistakes—cottage. His cottage mates include legless Wheels Potter, who gets around on a board with roller skates attached; Bighead Langhorn, who has a short, skinny body but a head the size of an enormous pumpkin; Cloud, a one-armed albino with a "massive head of curly white hair"; and Pill Suchanek, whose mother took a drug during her pregnancy that left Pill with flippers for arms. The teacher is named Robert but nicknamed Robot because "his only facial expression was a smile, his only mood cheerful" (*Little*, 18–19). Of course Miss Lake disapproves of this dark humor and scolds, "Don't call Albert 'Cloud.' . . . His name is Albert Werman." Cloud insists that he likes the name because before he came to Twin Oaks he was "Albert Worm, or just plain Wormy" (*Little*, 63), a nickname that reappears in three other books.

Typical of the group's wordplay and attitude is the nickname Sara Lee, which they use to refer to all those who do not live in Miss Lake's cottage. The name is an acronym for Similar And Regular And Like Everyone Else, a succinct expression of a theme that Kerr had already explored in *I'll Love You When You're More Like Me*. Kerr names her society for dwarfs The American Diminutives or TADpoles. She calls the organization for their parents PODS, for Parents of Diminutives. Larry La Belle refers to Little Little's contrasting suitors as Mr. Clean (also known as Mr. White Suit) and The Roach. Little Little's sister is called Cowboy because she was "supposed to have been the long-awaited boy, Larry La Belle, Jr." (*Little*, 13) and she started riding horses before her feet could even reach the stirrups. Cowboy's boyfriend is the teenage son of a Japanese entrepreneur. He is nicknamed Mock Hiroyuki, which looks and sounds right for a Japanese name, but there's nevertheless something amusing about it. Is he a mock boyfriend? He does not act much like a real one. Or perhaps because he is in the process of becoming Americanized, he is now only mock Japanese. Maybe he is a mock hero or a yucky hero.

The serious issues in *Deliver Us from Evie* are lightened by the playful names of Sheriff Starr and his freckle-faced son called Spots. Unbeknownst to Doug's vegetarian girlfriend Bella Hanna, the Burrmans show their disapproval by referring to her as Anna Banana. Angel Kidder is the religious but fickle girl that Parr has a crush on, whereas Cord Whittle is the boy who wants to tie Evie down to life on the farm and perhaps also whittle Patsy down to size. At church when the Lord's Prayer is being recited, Cord says "in this loud voice, 'Deliver us from Evie,' " after which he nudges Evie and laughs as if has made a good joke (*Evie*, 91). When big brother Doug does not want Cord invited to Thanksgiving dinner, he responds to his mother's defense of Cord as "a good farmer" with "Yeah, well Melvin's got more sense!" Readers soon learn that Melvin is the family's mule, who, Evie claims, will "work patiently for ten years for the chance to kick you once hard" (*Evie*, 14).

As a reminder of how important the Duff family is to the Burrman's community, their name keeps popping up not only on the thousand-acre Duffarm, but also on the Dufton School and the Duffton Municipal Swimming Pool. To manifest Evie's feminist awareness, Kerr plays with the name of Patsy Duff's private school, the Appleman Academy. When Evie gets her shirt wet bobbing for apples at the Duff's Halloween party, Patsy provides an "Appleperson Academy" sweatshirt that Evie has to explain to her parents: "the students call it Apple*person* Academy, for fun. You know, Mom, you're supposed to say spokesperson for spokesman, and chairperson for chairman." Evie's Dad asks good-naturedly "Does that make us the Burrpeople?" (*Evie*, 11).

John Fell, the hero of Kerr's three mystery novels, was obviously named with an eye—and an ear—toward the possibility of double meaning as evinced in the book titles: *Fell*, *Fell Back*, and *Fell Down* and in such puns as those made when John first meets Nina Deems and tells her that "Everyone calls me Fell."

> "As in fell down, fell apart, fell to pieces?"
> "Or fell back on or fell on one's feet—it doesn't all have to be negative."
> "Fell in love," she said. "Yeah, I guess there are good ways to fall, too . . . or you wouldn't be here."[1]

A big part of the plot in all three *Fell* books is the secret Sevens Club, a name that implies the members are lucky—as indeed they are in being granted an unbelievable number of extra privileges at the elite Gardner prep school. The deepest secret of all is how the members are chosen. The first thing each new student does when he comes to Gardner is to participate in a tree planting ceremony that includes choosing a name for the tree he plants. Those who happen to choose a name with seven letters— Madonna, Cormier, or even Up Yours—are tapped for membership. John had named his tree Good-bye. One reason was that he had recently expressed the opinion to his girlfriend, Keats, that her architect-father had been pretentious in naming their home Adieu, in honor of the fact that it was the last house he was going to design. Fell thought the sentiment could have been expressed just as well with plain old "Good-bye." Another reason for Fell's choice was that he liked the symbolism in his coming to Gardner disguised as Thompson Pingree; by participating in this ruse he was saying good-bye to his old name, his old life, and his old friends. That the boy he is substituting for is called Ping fits the boy's situation of being bounced around the world as part of the game his parents are playing.

Before coming to Gardner, Fell worked at the Plain and Fancy gourmet shop. One morning he forgets to put the raisins in their famous White Raisin Dream cakes. Capitalizing on his forgetfulness, he frosts and renames them "Remembering Helen" in honor of his girlfriend, Keats, whose real name was Helen J. Keating. "What the hell does that mean?" barks the owner. Fell patiently explains that the cakes are selling well: "People like kinky names on things." Then he suggests that they rename the Black Walnut cake to something like "Smiles We Left Behind Us," the enigmatic name that Ping's mother had given to one of her desolate paintings. Fell's unimpressed boss responds with "We're not in show biz here. . . ." (*Fell*, 55–56).

Because of the disclaimer in the preface of *ME ME ME ME ME*, "I've changed some names and details of other people involved," it is hard to know which bits of name play in that book are taken from memory and which are the result of the linguistic skill that Kerr developed in a lifetime of writing—most are probably instances of the latter. From the journal her father kept, she quotes, "Our daughter is dating the local undertaker's son, Donald Dare, tall, dark, and harmless. Dares very little is my guess"

(*ME*, 9). Marijane's father probably expressed a similar thought, but it was left to the writer, M. E. Kerr, to make up the alliterative name Donald Dare, which, in addition to the possible pun, sounds like Donald Duck.

In the second story in the book, "Where Are You Now, William Shakespeare?" Kerr has a 10-year-old boyfriend named William Shakespeare, called Billy for short. They both agree that if they ever marry and have a son they will name him Ellis (after her father) rather than William. Billy insists that this is not because William Shakespeare is a funny name; "it's just that there's a famous writer with the same name" (*ME*, 36).

In *Dinky Hocker Shoots Smack!* readers learn right away that Tucker's uncle is a "ding-a-ling." His "name was Guy Bell, but everyone called him Jingle, and he was not the type who minded" (*Dinky*, 28). On the day before Dinky starts a new diet, she buys herself two chocolate-dip ice cream cones and to her mother's horror explains to Tucker that she is gorging before she gets injected with a hormone made from pregnant women's urine. Each injection will cost five dollars and Dinky will get one shot a day. The hormone is amusingly named Follutin apparently from *fallopian* as in *tube* and *falutin* as in *high*.

When Dinky is feeling sorry for herself, she confides to the cat, "Dinky Dull and Nader Nowhere—that's us all right" (*Dinky*, 25). When Dinky's liberal father wants to deride the beliefs of Dinky's conservative friend, P. John, he calls him Eric Establishment. Significantly, P. John is the only one who calls Dinky by her given name of Susan rather than by the ironically insulting nickname of Dinky. Near the end of the book, Tucker, without giving the matter any thought, also begins calling her Susan, and P. John says "Thanks for finally calling her Susan." By drawing attention to this subtle change, Kerr prepares readers for the climax of Tucker's conversation with Dinky's father after the ordeal of the awards ceremony and the discovery of the graffiti. As Mr. Hocker's anger winds down, he looks at Tucker and asks, "And Susan's safely home?" "Tucker nodded and smiled slightly . . . not at Mr. Hocker, exactly; more at the soft sound, 'Susan' " (*Dinky*, 187). This is the clue that lets readers know Dinky is going to make it.

Linger gets its title from the Dunlinger family and their upscale Linger Restaurant, which the family is trying to make the social center of suburban Berryville. The underlying message of the name probably has something to do with the "lingering" effects, at least on the Peele family if not on the Dunlingers and the entire world, of the 1992 Gulf war. Kerr takes the irony of military terminology one step further when the soldier who is so beautiful that everyone calls him Movie Star is the one whose face is practically blown away by "friendly fire."

Another name of consequence to the plot was that of the tiny Mexican restaurant with the big pitchers of sangria and the "pretty little garden with the twinkling lights" (*Linger,* 50) that threatened to give the Dunlingers some competition. It was called Mañana until Bobby started the rumor that the owners caught cats in the fields near the canal and served them up as part of their well-spiced Mexican food. To make sure everyone got the message, he also used graffiti to change the name to "Mañana Meow" (*Linger,* 50).

In *I'll Love You When You're More Like Me,* television star Sabra St. Amour tells how her mother used to burst into her room, turn off Elvis, and say, "What are we doing lollygagging around here like Mrs. Average and her daughter, Mediocre? Let's go to the Apple for some fun!" (*Like Me,* 115) As Sabra explains, this was back in the "Dark Ages when Sam, Sam Superman" had them trapped in suburbia and Sabra's name was Maggie. Now that she is a big star, she and her mother can laugh at the old days, which are as different from their glamorous new life as the name Maggie Duggy is from Sabra St. Amour.

Kerr uses a different kind of a name change in *If I Love You, Am I Trapped Forever?* It is not the protagonist, however, who finally gets the right name; it is his nemesis, the boy he nicknamed Doomed. Alan is amazed when he hears his girlfriend, Leah, refer to Doomed as Duncan. When he expresses surprise, Leah says, "Alan you couldn't believe I *care* anything about Dunc!" As Alan observes, "From Doomed to Duncan to Dunc was a long distance in a very short space of time" (*Trapped,* 135–36). In *ME ME ME ME ME,* Kerr says that the boy who inspired this character was a Jewish refugee named Hyman Ginzburg. He got off to a bad start with his first name because in Auburn, "the word itself was never spoken unless you were talking privately about the wedding night." The other students called him "Hyman the Hopeless" or just plain "Hopeless" (*ME*, 14).

In *Gentlehands*, Kerr openly acknowledges the importance she places on names. She uses Skye Pennington's high-sounding name (high as the sky and penthouse) as the narrative hook to get readers interested in a romance between the boy who is telling the story and a girl who is out of his social class. The book begins with Buddy wondering what the summer would have been like if he had never met Skye Pennington. He muses:

> They always seem to have names like that, don't they? Rich, beautiful girls are never named Elsie Pip or Mary Smith. They have these special names and they say them in their particular tones and accents, and my mother was right, I was in over my head or out of my depth, or however she put it. (*Gentlehands*, 1)

The title of the book *Gentlehands* comes from the ironic name given to one of the most cruel Nazi SS guards at Auschwitz. The guard would taunt his Jewish prisoners from Rome by playing Puccini's opera *Tosca* and singing "O dolci mani," which translates as "gentle hands." The boy in the book has the plain name of Buddy Boyle, and his family is among those who refer to the Hadefield Country Club as the Hate-Filled Club, a pun that Kerr used earlier in *Love Is a Missing Person* and later in *Night Kites* to communicate the resentment that exists between ordinary townspeople and wealthy owners of seaside estates such as the Pennington's five acres named Beauregard. Buddy's father disgustedly refers to Skye as Miss Gottbucks from Beaublahblah. Even the names of the characters' pets give telltale evidence of social class. The Penningtons own Papillon (*butterfly* in French) dogs named Janice, January, and Little Ophelia. Buddy does not own a dog, but his upper-class grandfather has a keeshond named Mignon. Trenker says the name is taken from an opera, but a more gruesome interpretation is that it comes from *filet mignon*, a reminder of how Gentlehands used to turn selected prisoners over to his dogs.

When Skye introduces Buddy to her friends, he is surprised to meet a boy named "Connie as in Conrad." In Buddy's crowd, any boy with such a name would not have gone by this nickname. Toward the end of the book, Kerr manipulates the name Connie in a way that again highlights the differences in Skye's and Buddy's backgrounds. Skye tells Buddy that "Connie Spreckles has a new Connie." When Buddy does not understand, Skye explains, "A new Lincoln Continental." Buddy feels patronized when Skye adds, "Everybody calls them Connies" (*Gentlehands,* 170). This conversation takes less than half a page, but it is enough to let readers know that the leaves are beginning to fall on this summer romance.

The plot advances when Buddy's grandfather tells his social-climbing grandson that he needs "a man's name." Buddy cannot use his first name because then he would be confused with his father, so he decides to use his middle name, Raymond. He tells his best friend, Ollie, that he wants to be called Ray. Ollie at first feigns approval but then announces that, instead of being called Ollie, he wants to be called Gertrude. He raises his pant leg, flings his ankle back, and laughs loudly. The incident shows how naively Buddy accepts whatever his grandfather says and hints to readers that perhaps Buddy should follow Ollie's example and be a bit more skeptical.

A similar motif is used in the short story "Sunny Days and Sunny Nights." Marybeth's father winces when Sunny uses surfers' talk at the dinner table. To show his disapproval of the fun-loving Sunny, he asks him if he has a "real" name. When Sunny says "Harold," Marybeth's father responds, "That's not such a bad name, you can make Harry out of that . . . once he came right out and told Sunny that a man shouldn't have a boy's name" (*Sunny,* 219).

In *Love Is a Missing Person,* Suzy and Nan laugh hysterically at seeing Gwendolyn Spring's nameplate and realizing how close yet how far apart are "Miss G. Spring" and "Miss G. String" (*Missing,* 34). In *The Son of Someone Famous,* the students mock their teacher, Ella Early, by chanting "Ella Late who has no fate." In *Him She Loves?* the fattest boy in the social problems class is assigned to play the role of an anorexic called Anna Rexy, and the biggest midyear social event is the Dead of Winter Dance. Although people are to come as someone dead, the music will be "Live from Ironing Bored" (*Him,* 84). In *What I Really Think of You*, Opal's overweight mother is constantly eating Good & Plenty licorice candy while insisting that she doesn't "care one way or the other. . . . I just like the name" (*Think,* 170).

In *Is That You, Miss Blue?* Cardmaker is a card, but the name earns no special comment. However, an explanation of her roommate's name is worked into the story to emphasize the differences in the backgrounds of most of the girls at the school who come from "old" families and occasionally girls from newly affluent families from mountain communities. The roommate's name is Cute Dibblee, "and Cute isn't a nickname either. She's got a sister called Sweet" (*Blue,* 33).

The girls call the headmistress APE because she signs disciplinary notes with the initials of her name, Anne P. Ettinger. The school's secret honorary society is the ELA, which represents nothing more exciting than the Episcopal Library Association, but the girls who are not invited to join express their resentment by saying the initials stand for Extra Lucky Asses.

The name Ernestine Blue is appropriate for the religious teacher, Miss Blue, because blue is a sacred color often associated with the Virgin Mary. The fact that the story's protagonist also has a color name, Flanders Brown, shows that the two have something in common, foreshadowing their special student/teacher relationship. One of the things that makes Flanders feel so guilty is that, after Miss Blue puts the crucifixion painting in the bathroom, the girls ridicule her by devising such nicknames as "O torn cheeks," "Thorn-brain," and "O fingers-nailed" (*Blue,* 31). One of the other teachers tells Flanders that she had gone to school with Ernestine Blue, who had been called Nesty and was chased by all the boys. In another reversal on a name, Miss Blue teaches her chemistry class about snob gases, those "that refuse to combine with anything else under any conditions." Miss Blue explains that, although their discoverer, Cavendish, had named such things as argon and neon "noble gases because of their elite quality, she preferred to think of them as the snobs" (*Blue,* 121).

Alert readers will be able to find other examples of interesting names in Kerr's books. They help her readers remember her characters' names and personalities and the roles they play. Sometimes a name hints at things too bizarre to say or establishes a particular tone or moves the plot along. But naming is primarily an opportunity for both author and reader to have fun. Kerr is so accustomed to coaxing double meanings out of the names she creates that she now does it almost subconsciously and sometimes surprises herself. Only after she read reviews did she realize what appropriate names she had given to Angel Kidder and Cord Whittle in *Deliver Us from Evie,* and only after she turned in the manuscript for *ME ME ME ME ME* did she make the connection between the word *me* and M. E. Kerr's initials.

7. Her Literary Style

Never discuss manifest knowledge. If you can't be original, be
silent.

from *The Son of Someone Famous*

M. E. Kerr breezes into teenagers' lives like an Auntie Mame—
more experienced and worldly than their friends and less uptight
and protective than their parents. Her literary style flatters
young readers because she makes them feel as though they are
respected party guests worthy of her wittiest and most charming
efforts.

Just as appearance, behavior, and choice of friends and belong-
ings combine to create personal style, literary style develops out
of the unique blending of all the choices an author makes when
telling stories. Kerr's lively style is what initially attracted critics
and young readers and what still makes her books stand out from
the thousands of others in high school libraries. At least with her
first half-dozen books (those written before *Gentlehands* and *Little Little*), the plots are no more original than those in myriads of
mass-produced books for young people, and her settings in various kinds of schools serve as unobtrusive backdrops. Although a
few of her characters are truly memorable, the great majority fall
into stereotypical groups simply because there are so many of
them. But, as a talented dancer makes the highest leaps and the
fastest turns appear easy, Kerr's humorous and irreverent tone
helps her achieve a free-flowing smoothness that encourages
readers to sit back and relax. This chapter will examine some of
her best-developed techniques.

The Telling Detail

The miscellaneous classes that Kerr took at the New School during the years she lived in New York, the interesting people she got to know, and the books and journals she constantly reads provide a wealth of knowledge from which she culls information that generates a healthy intellectual curiosity among her young readers.

All her life Kerr has used a mental magnet to collect surprising details that she tucks away for future use. Contributing to her success in presenting these items is her succinctness. In *Little Little* Kerr explains that her protagonist will "never stand taller on two legs than the family dog does on four" (*Little,* 13) and that Cowboy's boyfriend "clings to Cowboy like Saran Wrap to your fingers" (*Little,* 48). In *Love Is a Missing Person*, Suzy laments her own speaking in clichés by complaining, "I catch words and phrases like other people catch germs" (*Missing,* 2). In *Deliver Us from Evie* Parr explains that "You'd say Evie was handsome. You'd say Mom was pretty" (*Evie,* 3); in *Night Kites*, Erick introduces Nicki by saying that she was "seventeen going on twenty-five" (*Kites,* 3).

In *Linger*, Mrs. Dunlinger explains that she liked President Reagan because of the way he treated Nancy: "He always made me feel good when I'd see him getting out of the helicopter on the White House lawn. He always touched her, always" (*Linger,* 179).

In *Night Kites* Pete answers the phone and is scolded by the employment agency for not telling them that someone with AIDS was living in the house. This incident was inspired by a poignant situation in Kerr's hometown. The family whose Christmas party invitations had always been the most coveted could not get caterers, much less guests, to come to their home after word got out that their son had AIDS.

In *I Stay Near You*, Grandfather Dechepare dies one night. Someone then has to climb onto the roof of the house and bring down one of the tiles to the Basque grandmother to allow the corpse's spirit to escape from the dwelling and ascend to heaven.

In *I'll Love You When You're More Like Me*, however, Wally's little sister explains that "The dead are no different from you or me, they're just in another stage of development (*Like Me*, 147).

In *Love Is a Missing Person*, when Suzy first visits the house of her father and his young wife, Enid, she notices *The International Thesaurus of Quotations* held open by a book of matches. Written on the page next to a Charles Lamb quotation that Enid had used so inappropriately the night before was "Memorize for Suzy's visit" (*Missing*, 94). Suzy sympathizes with Enid, but Suzy's mother describes her as a "redheaded creature with orange toenails" who "thinks *Vogue* is a weekly. . . ." (*Missing*, 127).

Kerr's real-life police officer neighbor—the man who became the fictional father of Buddy in *Gentlehands*—contributed some detective-related information that helped to prompt her writing of the *Fell* books. Kerr was fascinated by his observation that people do not commit suicide with their glasses on. When jumping from a high place, they set their glasses aside or put them in a pocket. When police find a body wearing smashed glasses, they suspect the victim fell or was pushed. Kerr was also interested to know that, in spite of the high tech trucks and vans shown in movies and on television police shows, most surveillance is done from ordinary cars with the detective sitting under a cardboard box with slits for peep holes and a hot water bottle for a urinal.

Kerr is a continual name dropper as in *Dinky Hocker*, when Tucker's mother tells him that as an artist he is "a depressing Bosch." To his questioning, she responds with the full name Hieronymous Bosch and tells Tucker to look him up, which he does: "A Dutch painter known for his scenes of nightmarish tortures in hell at the hands of weird monsters" (*Dinky*, 9–10).

Quotations from Petrarch, Dostoyevsky, Tennessee Williams, and O. Henry, along with references to Thomas Wolfe, J. D. Salinger, and Dante, move the plot along in *If I Love You, Am I Trapped Forever?* Kerr's works also include several literary pieces from Duncan's *Remote* newspaper. However, because of the sheer numbers of these scholarly references, it is difficult to decide whether they constitute a strength or a weakness.

In *Is That You, Miss Blue?* readers are treated to snippets of Miss Blue's best lectures on Antoine Henri Becquerel, Pierre Curie, and Marie Sklodowska Curie. In case someone grows really interested, Kerr also mentions the names of Sir J. J. Thomson and Sir Ernest Rutherford.

In more than one book, Kerr alludes to the beautifully written and humble "Death-Cell Prayer of Mary, Queen of Scots." The situation is full of the kind of irony that Kerr likes. A person who is condemned to execution by her cousin is a model of love and forgiveness, at least in the prayer.

Point of View

Kerr imparts an immediacy to her stories by using a first-person point of view and by beginning with such atypical and therefore intriguing opening lines as:

> On the night of the Senior Prom, I was stood up by Helen J. Keating—"Keats" they called her in Seaville, New York. (*Fell*)

> Soon I would be laughed at on national television, and so in love I couldn't chew my food. . . . (*Him She Loves?*)

> One warm night in May, in the back of the hearse, while I was whispering "I love you. . . ." (*I'll Love You When You're More Like Me*)

> "Sydney," Mr. Palmer said, "you are on your way to becoming the most famous dwarf in this country. . . ." (*Little Little*)

In *What I Really Think of You*, Opal speaks directly to readers as though they are among the "haves" who attend Central High and make Opal feel like "some red, ugly pimple on the side of someone's face, coming to a whitehead, in plain view mortifying everybody" (*Think*, 95).

> If I was to say that finally Opal Ringer is going to tell you what
> she really thinks of you, would you laugh? You always used to
> laugh. I never had to do much more than just show up and you'd
> start nudging each other with grins starting to tip your mouths.
> (*Think*, 3)

This book illustrates Kerr's use of language both to set a mood
and to develop character. In keeping with her religious subject
matter, Kerr surprises readers by employing biblical language in
unexpected places, such as Opal's explanation of Bobby John's
failure in kidnapping Dr. Guy Pegler: "A time to be born and a
time to die, as the Bible tells it; a time to plant, and a time to
pluck up that which is planted; a time to kill, and a time to heal; a
time to break down . . . which is what happened to Bobby John's
car that night, with Guy Pegler in it" (*Think*, 193).

When Bobby John confesses to Opal that he assisted in arranging
"the miracle," he and Opal drive through the countryside "with the
big moon beaming down, abundance of peace, said Psalms, so long
as the moon endureth" (*Think*, 98). The book closes with Opal and
Bud agreeing to pray for Jesse because it is something they can do
together without getting into trouble. As Opal explains, "Me and
him has seen the Devil's face, sweet nights when we slip, for there's
the sin in us same as there's the spirit" (*Think*, 208).

This is undoubtedly one of the most unusual allusions to sexual
activity in all of young adult literature. Its effectiveness lies in the
fact that readers are left to decide on the specifics. All they are
told is that it is enough to make Opal feel guilty—which, considering her background, could be nothing more than holding hands;
then again, it could be a great deal more.

Opal's mother tells her that "no one's going to buy the cow if he
can get the milk free" (*Think*, 133) and then urges her to quit trying to get all the answers when her head and heart have not yet
learned the same language. Kerr characterizes Mrs. Ringer as a
woman who secretly listens to Dolly Parton, Loretta Lynn, and
Crystal Gale "and would any day rather hear Loretta sing 'It
Wasn't God Who Made Honky Tonk Angels' than a whole heav-
enly choir sing 'Abide with Me' " (*Think*, 9).

Lively Dialogue

Although Kerr has said that she is not interested in writing movie or television scripts, she would be very good at it because she is a master at creating dialogue. Some of her sharpest lines occur in *ME ME ME ME ME* when Marijane says about Hyman and Ella Gwen's kissing, "They were wired for sound, and I was not even plugged in" (*ME,* 16). In *Night Kites,* when Nicki and Erick are swimming in the motel pool, Erick says "Somehow we got down to the shallow end, where we could touch, and that was what we did. We touched" (*Kites,* 144). In *Frankenlouse,* when Nick's mother is leaving for New York, Nick asks her "What's going on?" She answers, "I am, I'm going on. . . ."(*Frankenlouse,* 21).

Thumbing through Kerr's books, one seldom sees a page of type uninterrupted by quotation marks. Some pages look almost like a script. Take, for instance, the scene from *Him She Loves?* where Henry sneaks away from his restaurant work to telephone Valerie. It is Valentine's night, and her father has just appeared on a late night talk show where he got big laughs talking about Henry as a mental case with sauerkraut breath. Valerie's grandmother, Mrs. Trump, is usually the one who answers the telephone at the Kissenwiser home:

> The phone rang once, twice.
> "You forgot Mom's orchid, too," Ernie [Henry's older brother] said.
> "Mom hasn't gone on yet. They were playing 'Schnitzelbank.' Didn't you hear everyone singing?"
> "Mom's going on any minute," Ernie said.
> Mrs. Trump said, "Hello?"
> "I'd like to talk to Valerie, please."
> "From the Restaurant?" Mrs. Trump said. "Is that you?"
> "From the Restaurant. Heinrich. Mental Case. Sauerkraut Breath. Yes. It's me. I'd like to talk to Valerie, please, Mrs. Trump."
> "Hoo-ha! You got some nerve saying what you'd like at forty-five minutes before midnight and she's got school tomorrow."
> "I've got school tomorrow, too."

"Talk at school, not in the middle of the night. We go to bed around here."

"Mrs. Trump," I said, "I know you just watched him on TV. I know you're not asleep."

"You're putting me to sleep." She actually snored into the mouthpiece. "There. I'm asleep."

Click.

"Henry, the apple pancakes need their coffee! *Now!*" (*Him*, 131–32)

This conversation illustrates how Kerr juggles several balls at the same time. First, the interruptions from big brother Ernie give readers the feeling of being in a noisy restaurant kitchen where they, along with Henry, are forced to divide their attention. The information that the band is playing "Schnitzelbank" and that everyone is singing adds to the noise level as well as reminding readers that this is a German restaurant where "the apple pancakes need their coffee! *Now!*" Readers have met Grandmother Trump on the telephone before so they recognize her "Hoo-ha!" and her abrupt, questioning manner. But still it is impressive how consistently Kerr distinguishes the speaking styles of even minor characters. A less skilled writer would be forced to clutter up such dialogues with "Mrs. Trump said," "Henry responded," and "Ernie shouted."

Fun with Language

Kerr's ability to zero in on revealing details of people's speech allows her to establish her characters' backgrounds efficiently. In *Love Is a Missing Person*, Suzy's father falls in love with a cocktail waitress who pronounces Oedipus "oh-ead-apuss" (*Missing*, 86). In *What I Really Think of You*, Bobby John, who is thanked for bringing a crippled girl into The Hand for healing, says modestly, "Well, I was her mintor all right." Reverend Ringer scoffs at his son's mistake by saying that he sounds as if he were in charge of her breath (*Think*, 66). In *Is That You, Miss Blue?* Flanders's Grandmother Brown offers her theory about the reason Flanders's mother ran away to establish her own life in New York City, "Many women can't resist Italian [which she pronounces "eyetalian"] men. I've seen it in the movies" (*Blue,* 160).

When Flanders left the gracious southern speech patterns that surrounded her at Charles School and arrived at her mother's New York apartment house, she must have experienced culture shock. There she was greeted by the building superintendent:

> "I don't know no Ruth Brown."
> "Ruth Deacon?"
> "Miss Deacon? Yea, but she ain't got no daughter your age. She ain't got no daughter, period, that I know about."
> "Why would I lie?"
> "Why do pigs whistle, miss? Don't waste my time. Miss Deacon's at work."
> "Where?"
> "You're her daughter but you don't know where she works? Cute."
> "I'm her daughter," I said.
> "I'm her nephew, miss; I'm her great-grandpa. But I don't go inside her apartment when she ain't home."
> "Can I wait here in the lobby?"
> "Free country." He ducked back inside his apartment and shut the door. (*Blue,* 152)

In *Frankenlouse,* Aaron—a mute student—has a machine that he programs to do his speaking. This provides Kerr with an opportunity to use a different kind of speaking style, as in the *Fell Down* chapters supposedly written by the ventriloquist's dummy. One of Kerr's more subtle techniques is changing the speech patterns of her characters as an indication of growth. P. John Knight in *Dinky Hocker Shoots Smack!* comes into the story with a chip on his shoulder. Readers first meet him in a creative writing class where he reads his poem "Thanks to the United Nations."

> Aren't you glad the Chinese are in the U.N. now?
> Oh boy? And how!
> Who wants to live forever?
> Do you? Do I? Welcome, slant-eye . . . (*Dinky,* 45)

When the teacher observes that his 13 lines are more politics than poetry, P. John responds with:

> All great poets mix politics with poetry: Yevtushenko, Joel Oppenheimer, Pablo Neruda."
> "Who's Pablo Neruda?" Mr. Baird asked.
> P. John heaved an exasperated sigh. "He *only* won the Nobel Prize for 1971, Professor!" (*Dinky,* 45)

P. John continues in this manner all through the winter, finally leaving Brooklyn Heights and going away to an experimental school. When he comes back for a surprise visit to Dinky, it is Dinky who has the chip on her shoulder. When she refuses to apologize as her mother demands, P. John's new maturity is obvious in his simple statement, "Let her go. I don't think she needs a surprise like this" (*Dinky,* 175).

Kerr's fondness for words is evident in the way she plays with rhymes and rhyming. Reminiscent of how the parrot in *The Shuteyes* was named Lornge as a counter to the old statement that nothing rhymes with orange, in *Frankenlouse* the new boyfriend of Nick's mother gives her a bracelet from Tiffany's inscribed with the words "Silver, month, window, orange, plinth, false, depth, chimney, swamp." When she does not immediately grasp their significance, he tells her to look at the card where he has written, "Just as there is no rhyme for any of these words in the English language, there is no match for you. . . ." (*Frankenlouse,* 116).

In *Dinky Hocker*, Natalia Line, Dinky's cousin, changes her speech patterns depending on how psychologically comfortable she feels. When nervous or upset, she speaks in rhyme. In other books, characters rhyme just for fun. In *ME ME ME ME ME*, Marijane the Spy and her friends have a rhyming dialogue they use to tease the new girl in town about her mother's job: "You have to be very very quicket to take a ticket" (*ME,* 52). In *Gentlehands*, as Buddy Boyle is going off to read his Grandfather's farewell message, his boss lightens the somber moment by admitting that he plans to escape life's harsh realities: "Grass will put

At the Margaret A. Edwards awards luncheon in July of 1993, M. E. Kerr was honored by the American Library Association for having written books that help young adults "to grow and understand themselves and their role in society."

you on your ass and make time pass" (*Gentlehands,* 164). When Buddy and Skye smoke the marijuana that Buddy took out of the wastebasket at the Sweet Mouth, Kerr uses a rhyming dialogue to communicate their pleasurable, sensual feelings and to prepare readers for the tender love scene that follows.

In *The Shuteyes*, Chester Dumbello's mother makes fun of the Edgar A. Guest rhymes that Rita Box-Bender recites, but when she predicts the future for her clients, she adds to the mystique by speaking in rhyme herself:

> Someone you know is going away,
> Maybe today, maybe today,
> Someone you'll miss is saying goodbye,
> I don't know why, you don't know why. . . . (*Shuteyes,* 25)

On the planet of Alert, Chester apologizes for forgetting that his name had been changed. Mr. Lyric, the English teacher, says helpfully, "That's not much of a trick. You are now Chester Quick" (*Shuteyes,* 43).

Kerr is also fascinated with the arbitrariness of language. A linguistic quirk that she would like to use is that English has only three words beginning with *dw*: *dwarf, dwell,* and *dwindle.* Perhaps the oddness of the sound is what contributed to its use in the newly invented *dweeb,* slang for *nerd* or *jerk.*

Foreign languages are interesting to Kerr's characters. In *The Son of Someone Famous,* Adam ponders what his grandfather told him about the Chinese symbol for the word *crisis* being composed of a character representing danger and another representing opportunity. Kerr begins one of The Mouth's chapters in *Fell Down* with:

> In tennis love means zero and in Sanskrit it means trembling elbows.
> It surprised Lenny how fast and how much Nels liked him.
> Adored him, truly. Zero . . . Trembling elbows. (*Fell Down,* 48)

When Little Little and her sister are discussing what Mrs. La Belle calls bickering, Little Little confesses that she thinks by being born a dwarf, she ruined the charmed life her parents led in their youth. Cowboy argues that it was simply that her parents grew up, "Nothing good begins with 'adult.' There's adult, adulterate, adultery. . . ." (*Little,* 77).

No character expounds linguistic insights better than Wally in *I'll Love You When You're More Like Me.* His teacher, Mr. Sponzini, says he would make a good etymologist or linguist, but Wally's father does not appreciate it when Wally quotes—in Latin—Pliny the Elder on the similarities between orchids and testicles. Nor does his mother appreciate the essay he writes on linguistic evasions inspired by her euphemisms for death. Wally's essay explains that in Madagascar people avoid the word *lightning* lest it strike and that Russian peasants try to placate their enemy the bear by calling it "honey eater." In Hungary, furthermore, mothers of new babies used to maintain that their offspring were ugly in order to avoid arousing the jealousy of evil spirits.

Interesting Comparisons

Kerr uses metaphors both to create vivid pictures and to develop characterization. In *Love Is a Missing Person,* Miss Spring has been forced to admit to herself that the man she has loved all these years isn't worthy of her affections. She complains to Suzy, who is all caught up in her sister's running away:

> I don't give a tinker's dam, honey, what is going down the road right now. All I know is that I'm a car wreck smack-dab in the middle, broken and bleeding and, more's the pity, still drawing deep breaths. How many times am I going to be run over by the rest of you out driving in your big hurries? (*Missing,* 134)

In *I'll Love You When You're More Like Me*, Sabra St. Amour's stage mother reveals her brassy, New York personality when she counsels Sabra, "You're not just another salami decorating the deli ceiling—you're special" (*Like Me,* 115). To Fedora, the director of Sabra's show, who comes to the beach house and begins to hint coyly at new plans, Madame St. Amour says, "I wish you'd pee or get off the pot, because the suspense is killing yours truly" (*Like Me,* 50). Kerr writes that Fedora winced at the vulgarity, which tells readers something about Fedora and at the same time protects Kerr from those who might criticize her for writing such slang. She has at least acknowledged its inappropriateness.

During a bad rainstorm in *Deliver Us from Evie,* Parr confesses to Angel that he was partially responsible for hanging the infamous sign about Patsy and Evie on the veterans' monument. Erick figures that the heavens must have liked hearing his confession because of the "claps of thunder" he got for telling it (*Evie,* 157).

The appeal of Kerr's comparisons is their basis in everyday material familiar to teenagers. For example, Opal Ringer reveals how estranged she feels from the other teenagers by stating, "You never changed me, just made me dig deeper under my strangeness, made me pull the crazy blanket over my head to look out at your real world through eye slits" (*Think*, 4).

When Buddy comes down to The Hand and squeezes in to sit by Opal, he looks at her in a way that gives new meaning to the choir's song, "When love shines in, how the heart is turned to singing." Opal is filled with such good feelings that, to her surprise, she is "slain in the spirit." She comes up singing, the way she always thought she could but not in any language she ever heard before:

> Just as loud and in my own voice, soaking wet all over me, cameras going, I could see their red eyes on me, tiny red living specks, and I had tongues. I felt my body giving room to my soul while it burst into full bloom. (*Think*, 197)

In *I'll Love You When You're More Like Me*, Wally Witherspoon is unofficially engaged to Harriet Hren, but Lauralei Rabinowitz keeps returning to his thoughts "like mildew you can't get off a suitcase no matter how often you set it out in the sun" (*Like Me*, 4). He has fallen in love with Lauralei "the way a storm rages, or a rock number builds, the way you fly in dreams all by yourself, or go down a roller coaster smiling while you're screaming" (*Like Me*, 7).

Foreshadowing

Another of Kerr's strengths is the foreshadowing with which she prepares her readers. Even though they may not know exactly what is going to happen, they have a sense of satisfaction at the end—a feeling that things worked out as they should have. For example, early in *Gentlehands* readers are warned that things are not always as they appear when Skye and Grandpa Trenker are talking about birds. She says, "I really admire birds, they're so *free*. I mean they *symbolize* freedom." Trenker explains that this is a false notion because birds cannot move from one area to another. They are very restricted, "prisoners, really, of their own territory" (*Gentlehands,* 24). Trenker's description could as easily have been of himself as of the birds. Although to Skye and Buddy, he appears to have everything, he is very much a prisoner of his past. His freedom of movement is so limited that, when he is forced to change locations, he ironically describes himself as a package being sent somewhere. A second warning about things not being what they appear is contained in a lesson Trenker gives Buddy in self-confidence: "You can become anything you want to be," he tells Buddy. "It's a matter of authority. Whatever a man's confidence, that's his capacity" (*Gentlehands,* 116). That Trenker sincerely believes this and has apparently had experiences that taught it to him, prepares readers to accept the conclusion of the book.

Early in *Him She Loves?* the fate of Valerie's and Henry's relationship is foreshadowed. Kerr shows the temporary nature of young romances when Henry's first-day conversation with Valerie is interrupted by a phone call from his previous girlfriend. She is remembering last New Year's Eve and wants to know if he is remembering, too. When he begins telling her about Valerie Kissenwiser and her famous father, she says, "I'm glad I called because now I know for once and for all it's over" (*Him,* 19). Henry's response is that it was finished a year ago at Christmas. Henry had paid $165 for a ring, but he had spoiled the romance of the moment by accompanying the gift with an explicit statement that in no way was it to be considered an engagement ring. The girlfriend had responded with the kind of grand gesture that most women dream about but cannot bring themselves to make. She threw it out the window of the taxi.

Even the title of *If I Love You, Am I Trapped Forever?* lightly portends the end of Leah and Alan's romance. A stronger hint lies in Alan's words:

> Whenever I feel great, I think something's going to happen as punishment. I'll go blind or deaf or wake up from the dream.

> That afternoon I decided my punishment would be that I'd
> flunk Latin and not graduate with my class. I made a dive for
> my book bag.
>   That was when I found it. (*Trapped,* 116)

What he found was a letter from Duncan to Leah, which indeed
foretold the end of their love relationship.

Another incident is suggested when Alan tells Mrs. Stein that
he has become so mature he does not remember the past. She
smiles and wistfully advises him that those who do not remember
the past are condemned to relive it. These words jump back into
the readers' minds when Mrs. Stein runs away with the alcoholic
football coach. She apparently plans to rescue him from his alcoholism just as she had rescued Mr. Stein a decade earlier.

Observations about Things That Matter

Young readers ignore many writers whose skill is equal to, or
greater than, Kerr's. They pay attention to Kerr's books because
she writes about topics and feelings that concern teenagers: family, religion, socioeconomic differences, personal feelings, male /
female disagreements, and the setting of life goals.

Because teenagers are taking their first steps toward independence from their families, they appreciate glimpses into the
ways other families relate to each other. In *ME ME ME ME
ME*, Marijane confesses that she was glad her boarding school
was a long way from home and that because of the war, travel
was curtailed and her family would not be coming to visit and
humiliate her.

> Why did my mother wear so much junk jewelry? Why did my
> father have to say things like "Soup's on!" instead of "Dinner's
> ready," or "How do?" instead of "How do you do?" Why did my
> mother have to mention the price of everything, and talk about
> "bargains?" Why didn't we ever have wine with dinner, or go to
> concerts, and why did my father have to call classical music
> "long-hair noise?" (*ME,* 133)

Kerr shows young readers they are not the only ones who have such feelings of embarrassment. In *What I Really Think of You*, every Sunday Opal is irritated with her preacher father. After the family comes home from church, while she and her mother prepare dinner, he goes into his room and prays out loud about all the things sitting "heavy on his head like a basket of wet wash." If they are having a dinner guest, Opal feels as embarrassed as she would "going to the toilet with the door open" (*Think*, 170). Once, after Opal had asked permission to go to a costume party, Reverend Ringer prays that Opal will "cast her eyes from this godless astrology." Opal's mother, Arnelle, tries to smooth her feelings and tell her not to be critical of her father, but then the prayer goes on, "Jesus, help Arnelle fight Satan's gluttony so's she can sing your praises once again before our humble flock, guide her from. . . ." Opal's mother isn't nearly as understanding about this prayer, and Opal cannot resist adding to her mother's discomfort by saying, "Shoe's on the other foot now" (*Think*, 172).

In *If I Love You, Am I Trapped Forever?* the conflict is more subtle. Alan explains how his grandfather is a put-down artist— not the kind who would say anything like "Alan, you stupid clown, nobody wants to read anything you'd write!" Instead he says things like, "Well, it's a big undertaking. I hope you can pull it off" and "Just remember, you put all that time and money into the boat you were going to build, and nothing came of *that* either" (*Trapped*, 2).

In *Night Kites*, Nicki tells the boys they have to come over and meet her father before the two couples go into New York for the weekend. As it turns out, her father is out of town, and she later confesses to Erick, "I made all that up about Daddy wanting to meet all of you before we all went into New York City. . . . I knew that was what you all expected, that Daddy'd want to look you over" (*Kites*, 143).

In *What I Really Think of You*, when Jesse Pegler accuses Seal Von Hennig of being a P. K. groupie, Kerr is letting Jesse accuse his family of being in show business rather than religion since actors and singers are usually the ones with "groupies."

Kerr's bravery in including references to religion can be appreciated only when one recognizes how neglected God and religion are in teenage fiction. Most authors ignore such matters for fear of offending members of particular groups or of losing sales because teachers and librarians may think they should not spend public funds on material with religious overtones. The absence of religion from young adult books is especially unrealistic since for many people the teenage years are the ones in which they spend the most time and energy thinking about and discussing religion. As part of their developing independence, they have to make religious decisions, deciding for example whether to stay with the faith (or nonfaith) of their parents; whether to approach religion as whole-hearted believers, skeptics, or something in between; and whether to limit their dating to members of their own church.

Kerr understands these dilemmas, and, although not pointing her audience toward any particular belief or nonbelief system, she communicates that religious matters deserve some prime-time thinking. In her first book, Dinky Hocker cleverly announces that the biblical theme for the day is boredom. When Tucker argues that "There's nothing about boredom in the Bible," Dinky responds that he would not know since he and his family "only show up in church once a year." Finally Dinky explains that her biblical theme is taken from Hebrews 13:8, "Jesus Christ the same yesterday, and today, and forever" (*Dinky,* 146).

The morning after the family's health food store burns, Tucker writes P. John that they are all going to church and "pray like mad for a miracle." At church the minister intones, "Almighty God, the fountain of all wisdom, who knowest our necessities before we ask, and our weaknesses before we sin; we beseech thee to forgive and have compassion upon our infirmities. . . ." Tucker looks over at his uncle and cannot determine if his face is so red because of the references to weaknesses, forgiveness, and infirmities or because he has his usual Sunday-morning hangover (*Dinky,* 125).

In *Is That You, Miss Blue?,* there is the obvious irony of Miss Blue's dismissal from teaching at a church-sponsored school because she is "too" religious. Several scenes show how deprived Cardmaker is because her father's ministerial salary does not stretch far enough to buy her a winter coat or a party dress. After the big dance of the year, Cardmaker is punished for being found in the bathroom with a boy. All she was trying to do was wash off the purple that had gotten on her neck from her newly dyed but very old dress. She would rather be expelled from school than confess the truth to her father, who already feels guilty about being a poor provider.

The family's financial situation developed when Cardmaker's father took it upon himself to point out things he was dissatisfied with in the church, and a certain Right Reverend (who took the "right" in his title literally) had him transferred to the poorest parish in New Jersey. This leaves Cardmaker fuming over "a bunch of phonies living off stories of Jesus," a poor man who did not even have a title but today is represented by men "hustling to get the rich parishes with the big houses and the long black cars" and wanting "to be the Right Reverend this and the Holiness that. . . ." (*Blue*, 86).

A running argument between the girls about atheism and agnosticism gives Kerr the opportunity to bring in opposing opinions. When Flanders says that she is "maybe an agnostic," Cardmaker responds, "That's wishy-washy, spineless, and dull" (*Blue*, 141). Cardmaker starts an atheist club, whose members show their allegiance by singing the required hymns backward. Flanders argues with one of the members:

> "How can you be an atheist when your mother owns a white Mercedes?" I said.
> "A Mercedes has nothing to do with God."
> "How can you *not* believe in God with all you have?" I persisted. "Atheism is for have-nots and malcontents."
> "You know nothing about atheists," she said. "A lot of us are worth fortunes."
> "Way your it have." I shrugged. (*Blue*, 94)

By topping off a scene with a little joke like Flanders's reversed speech, Kerr makes serious points without leaving readers feeling preached at. She also lets her characters go away with varying opinions. Although Cardmaker finally decides to "take God back," Flanders's attitudes appear to remain basically the same.

Although critics have pointed to the skepticism displayed by some of Kerr's characters and her negative observations about TV evangelism, Kerr laments that her positive portrayals of ministers go unnoticed; they are simply taken for granted. In *Little Little*, Grandfather La Belle, a Methodist minister, is "the one sensible person in the book"—the only one smart enough to see that Little Little cannot be kept under glass her whole life. In *Night Kites*, Reverend Shorr stands up against the membership rules of the prejudicial Hadefield Club and is the only member of the community who befriends Pete and comes on a regular basis to play backgammon with him.

In the *Fell* books, Kerr's knowledge and interest in psychology appears in Mrs. Pingree's esoteric explanation that "recurring dreams are those that wake the dreamer and cause him to learn instead of unlearn them. A recurring dream is a kind of neurological flypaper" (*Fell*, 44). In *Fell Down*, the insights are more prosaic but probably more useful. After Fell and his mother quarrel on the phone, they apologize to each other and he tells her where he is calling from and why, "But it wasn't an easy conversation. Once you've spit out a lot of venom at each other, it's hard to just get past it" (*Fell Down*, 55). A few pages later, he writes, "Every time I caught myself doing anything fun and familiar, I marked it, telling myself I was back and okay. But I was suspicious of the idea at the same time. If I really was back and okay, how come I was so conscious of it?" (*Fell Down*, 65).

In *Love Is a Missing Person*, Miss Spring advises Suzy to read *Member of the Wedding* because "It's all about a young girl getting caught up in her brother's wedding, so caught up in it she was losing her own identity." Suzy argues that she is not having such a problem, "though sometimes I think I wouldn't mind if I was" (*Missing*, 82).

In *The Shuteyes*, Chester asks his mother why she gives such unhappy interpretations for all of the dreams her clients bring to her. She explains, "Chester, people don't come back to hear happy stuff. People like mystery. Even that poor little child needs some mystery in her life, or she'll end up talking to herself in the doorways of downtown stores someday" (*Shuteyes,* 26).

Kerr puts into words many of the vague feelings that her readers do not have the sophistication to describe. Yet, when they read something like Brenda Belle's confession of insecurity in *The Son of Someone Famous,* they experience a jolt of recognition. Brenda Belle is puzzling over why Adam Blessing seems to like her and sadly concludes that it is because there is something wrong with him. He was probably expelled from school because he is "slightly crazy . . . whacked out." This depresses Brenda Belle because she was looking for "normal companionship, not a misfit. I wanted someone who fit, so I'd feel I fit, too" (*Famous,* 48).

There's really nothing wrong with Adam's head, but he, too, is suspicious about his relationship with Brenda Belle—they are never affectionate with each other except in public. When he tells his grandfather he guesses he feels sorry for Brenda, Mr. Blessing responds, "Don't let that be the only reason you want to see a girl. When you pity someone, sometimes all it means is you wish someone would pity you"(*Famous,* 32).

When Adam overhears his veterinarian grandfather giving out free advice over the telephone, he suddenly feels a surge of love for the old man "because no matter what life had done to him, he wasn't mean." This impresses Adam because he imagines that life has few goodies in story for him, too, and he is unsure whether he can make it through without being mean. There have been times when he felt the meanness creeping into his soul, times when he "wanted to hurt someone, wanted someone to have a party where no one would show up . . . things like that" (*Famous,* 58).

Kerr encourages her readers to look behind the surface structure of even the simplest actions. In *I'll Love You When You're More Like Me,* Wally, Charlie, and Harriet see Sabra at the local beach hangout, and Harriet sends Wally over to ask Sabra for a dance. Wally ponders "I'm not sure whether Harriet wanted to impress other people with the fact I'd met her, or whether she wanted to sit out a set with Charlie so he wouldn't leave us without wheels" (*Like Me,* 79).

In *Frankenlouse*, the resentment that Nick feels toward his mother's new boyfriend is illustrated by the silent exchange that takes place when the boyfriend gives Nick a copy of *My Life as a Cartoonist* by Harvey Kurtzman, the founder of *Mad* magazine. "'Thanks, Sam,' I said. My eyes said: *You can't buy your way in . . . !* His blinked back: *That's what you think!*" (*Frankenlouse,* 117)

In *Is That You, Miss Blue?* Flanders is feeling guilty about making fun of Miss Blue and says,

> I had the feeling if I laughed any longer I'd have some terrible punishment inflicted on me, because I had the feeling what I was doing was cruel. My father had told me once that often if you did something cruel, you hurt yourself, had a trivial accident, or missed an appointment you looked forward to—as a way of making yourself pay for the cruelty. (*Blue,* 113)

Feminist observations and questions frequently find their way into Kerr's books. Marijane learns her first lesson in the power of boys, according to *ME ME ME ME ME*, at Laura Bryan's ballroom dancing school where

> You couldn't even get out on the floor without a boy choosing you for a partner. If a boy didn't choose you, you were a wallflower, which was a poor wretch, all dressed up, sitting by herself on the sidelines in a folding chair, pretending she was fascinated by her own hands.
> Boys were never wallflowers. (*ME,* 61)

Suzy arrives at a new level of awareness in *Love Is a Missing Person* when she realizes that her father never asks about Suzy's sister, Chicago. Instead he is only concerned with how Chicago feels about him, "as though apart from that she had no existence which was of any importance" (*Missing,* 100).

In *What I Really Think of You*, Seal von Hennig gets her nickname from becoming the St. Francis of Seaville High when she dates Eddie Eden, whose father runs an animal preserve. "Seal always got gung ho on any subject that interested the boy she was dating. She was known for that around Seaville" (*Think,* 17).

Kerr almost seems to feel sorry for her when she loses her next P. K. boyfriend by interrupting a long, passionate kiss to tell him about a new idea she has for telephone tithing.

Brenda Belle Blossom, in *The Son of Someone Famous*, takes her sort-of boyfriend a newly sprouted sweet potato plant with the explanation:

> "Since we're going steady, now, I'm teaching you about beautiful things . . . since I'm not a beautiful thing."
>
> "I don't get you, Brenda Belle."
>
> "This will become a beautiful thing, but after it's a beautiful thing for a while, it'll change," I said.
>
> "How will it change?"
>
> "It'll begin to stink," I said. "It will make you realize that beauty is not that big a deal, just in case you wish you were going steady with a beauty contest winner." (*Famous*, 90)

Brenda Belle and her mother argue about personal style and motherhood when Brenda Belle's mother draws comparisons between Brenda and her Aunt Faith, who in her youth "was very busy being the smart aleck, slapping her knees when she laughed, getting to her feet in company to mimic someone," just never thinking how she looked to boys. Aunt Faith finally married, but her husband "never gave her a child." Brenda explains, "My mother always said a man *gave* a woman a child, as though the woman had no part in its conception" (*Famous*, 60–61).

The irony of this attitude is stronger when viewed in connection with what happens in *Is That You, Miss Blue?* The most popular girl in school, France Shipp, does not come back after Christmas. The rumor is that she is pregnant, but her boyfriend is back at the neighboring boys' school, "as handsome as ever, showing no signs of being involved. . . ." (*Blue*, 166).

Little Little is negatively impressed that when Tom Thumb died he was buried in a big, fancy vault with a grandiose epitaph, whereas right next to it on Lavinia Thumb's vault, the only message was "His Wife," not even her name. Lavinia had been two inches shorter than Tom. When Little Little asked her grandfather where all the famous female dwarfs were, "he said they were buried in history along with other notable ladies" (*Little,* 25). She finds one, however, to write her senior research paper on: Lia Graf, the 27-inch circus performer who had her picture taken sitting on the lap of J. P. Morgan when he was testifying before the Senate Banking Committee. "She came to a sad end in a Nazi concentration camp, doomed not only because she was a Jew but also because she was a dwarf" (*Little,* 175).

Rather than dwelling on such matters, Kerr shines a light on them momentarily and then moves on to something else, leaving readers to draw their own conclusions. And when it is deserved, she will throw in a counterargument to balance the scales. The best example is in *I'll Love You When You're More Like Me.* Wally reminds his little sister "for the umpteenth time" that she could be the one to carry on the family mortuary business. She responds that she plans to be "an internationally renowned poet, and besides it isn't woman's work." "Where," Wally asks, "is women's liberation when I need it?" (*Like Me,* 44).

In Kerr's recent books (*Deliver Us from Evie, Night Kites, Frankenlouse,* and the *Fell* series), the mothers are much more fully developed and presented more positively than in her earlier books, in which celebrity fathers received the lion's share of attention. But even in those earlier works, there are positive role models. Whereas the portrayal of Dinky Hocker's mother is almost too negative to be credible, Tucker's mother is an appealing blend of common sense, understanding, and ambition. After Tucker finds her weeping at the kitchen table where she has been studying for a law exam before going to her regular job at *Stirring Romance,* he expresses his amazement to Natalia that his mother wants to be something more significant than just his mother. A similar idea appears in *Is That You, Miss Blue?* when Flanders is giving her mother a sermon on parental responsibility and her mother says, "Flan, I have news for you. I didn't give up my right to individuality once I had you" (*Blue,* 156).

In *Love Is a Missing Person,* Suzy Slade's mother is a multifaceted character who at first seems frivolous, dressing to match her sunporch and wanting to prove that she can win back her husband even though she does not want him. But as the story progresses, we discover that she has considerable depth. She makes Suzy go to work at the library on the day that her sister runs away, explaining, "In a crisis, you do the same as you do every day. That's what holds things together. Routine is fiber, and in a crisis, fiber binds" (*Missing*, 141). Despite this brand of wisdom, Mrs. Slade does not become too wise or too good to be believed. She is catty about the woman her former husband decides to marry, and she resents the fact that one of her friends attributes the mismatch to love rather than to a psychotic condition on the part of Mr. Slade.

Many of the Kerr's subjects are also addressed in television sitcoms. However, the premise of most sitcoms is that change is bad whereas the status quo is good. Each show opens with a scene of normality, followed by the development of a problem. Actions taken by the characters, who attempt to solve the problem, only make it worse. Finally, when the situation appears hopeless, someone or something comes in from the outside and saves the day. Conditions return to normal, and the show closes with a scene depicting the characters in a position similar to the one they were in at the beginning.

Lawrence Mintz, professor of American studies at the University of Maryland, contends that, in the situation comedy, the family is never really threatened. The problems are always the result of miscommunication. The inherent, wish-fulfilling premise is that if people are honest and communicate clearly with each other, their problems will disappear. Some sitcoms will titillate viewers by mentioning a serious issue, but, in general, the show's writers skirt that issue by making a joke. When people laugh, they are not so frightened. The overall effect and the reason for the appeal of the situation comedy is that it lulls viewers into a false sense of security.[1]

Like the sitcoms, Kerr recommends honest communication to solve problems, and like the sitcoms she makes her readers laugh when a topic is uncomfortably solemn. However, a major difference is that she does not bring up a grave issue only to flit away from it with a joke. Her readers are well aware that Little Little's dwarfism is a real problem that is not going to go away, nor in *Night Kites* is there going to be a miraculous cure for Peter, no matter how candidly family members communicate nor how cleverly Kerr quips about his illness. In *Gentlehands*, no evidence— no surprise witnesses—come forth to prove that the story about Buddy's grandfather is a case of mistaken identity. In *If I Love You, Am I Trapped Forever?* Alan Bennett and Catherine Stein communicate wonderfully, but Alan still loses his girlfriend to Duncan, and Mrs. Stein still runs away with the football coach. Moreover, in *I Stay Near You*, even though Powell Storm and Mildred Cone are in love with each other, they do not get to marry and live happily ever after.

A second important difference between Kerr's books and situation comedies is that Kerr's protagonists do not circle around to end up at the same place they began. Early in the stories, they are preoccupied with themselves, but as the plots progress their views are enlarged and tempered by their experiences and interactions with others. Each book ends with the protagonist having arrived at a new level of maturity. For example, *What I Really Think of You* begins with Opal lamenting the hostility and the differences between herself and the "haves" who attend Seaville High. It ends with her expressing love for these same people: "When the Rapture comes, I want you all along, somehow, someway, every last one of you, ascending with me" (*Think*, 208). *The Son of Someone Famous* begins with Brenda Belle worrying about her lack of acceptance and popularity and ends with her mother observing, "I have this feeling, this very definite feeling that you are slipping away from the crowd—that you are losing interest in the things other girls in Storm care about" (*Famous*, 226). *Gentlehands* begins with Buddy Boyle willing to do anything to look and act like a part of Skye's crowd. It ends with him consciously deciding to leave the navy blue cashmere sweater that Skye had given him in a heap on the floor of his grandfather's house among the tangled tapes of *Madame Butterfly* and *La Traviata*. This symbolic gesture of leaving "everything about that summer behind me" illustrates a new acceptance of reality on Buddy's part (*Gentlehands*, 183).

Even in *I'll Love You When You're More Like Me*, which seems to end where it begins with Wally Witherspoon courting Lauralei Rabinowitz, a difference is that Wally is no longer planning to be a mortician. He has managed to make that break with his father's expectations, not an inconsiderable achievement.

A third difference between Kerr's books and typical sitcoms is that her characters solve their problems or adjust to them through their own actions. This may be as wish-fulfilling as the sitcoms, but at least the underlying premise is one of competence. Kerr's characters set an example of self-motivation. They take action instead of waiting passively to be rescued by the fates.

After reading an M. E. Kerr book and after watching a situation comedy, young adults may feel an equivalent sense of pleasure and security. But if Mintz's theory is correct, the feeling of security engendered by watching a situation comedy comes from the illusion that assistance will always come along in time to save the protagonists from real danger. In contrast, readers of Kerr's books gain a feeling of security from identifying with the success of the characters, who use their own wits and strengths to solve their problems and/or adjust to those things that cannot be changed.

8. Her Defense
of the Underdog

You were different-looking. Definitely. Maybe if you hadn't been, you'd have fared better in our small town, but I doubt it. . . .

from *ME ME ME ME ME*

Marijane's first memories of identifying with the underdog come from Sunday afternoons when her father would read aloud the novels of Charles Dickens. She went on to find American writers who sided with the disadvantaged or the excluded: Sherwood Anderson, Erskine Caldwell, William Faulkner, Carson McCullers, and John Steinbeck.

She grew up in an affluent home and had what by most standards would be considered a privileged childhood, yet she always identified with the outcast. In a "Books Remembered" column she wrote for the *Children's Book Council Features*,[1] she pondered why she was attracted to the deprived and why as a teenager the only thing that distinguished her from other teenagers was that she "wrote: stories, poems, chapters of novels . . . all about the disadvantaged and outcast."

The most memorable of the stories in *ME ME ME ME ME* is entitled "Marijane the Spy." It is a heart-chilling story of children's cruelty to someone who is different. The cruelty has snowballed into an avalanche too hard to stop by the time Marijane and her friends find out that the reason their new classmate, Millicent, dresses so neatly and carefully "in a little hat and gloves and shiny shoes" and that she turns in "the best compositions with the best penmanship and the straightest margins" is that she is trying so hard to look and be like anything but a convict's daughter. Millicent and her mother have come to Auburn, New York, to be near Millicent's father as he serves his term in the state prison. Kerr's statement in the afterword that "I think I felt my first real shame at how I'd treated someone, and I know that I thought of Millicent again and again as I grew up" (*ME*, 58) is worth dozens of the less believable stories and didactic messages that adults are so fond of dropping on teenage ears.

As Kerr uncovers the many faces of prejudice, her goal is not to sermonize but to help readers recognize that prejudice is a part of most people's lives and that overcoming it is a personal challenge. Thoughtful readers of *Dinky Hocker Shoots Smack!* will question their own prejudices against either political liberals or conservatives, fat people, those who have been in institutions for mental-health problems, and people who have been on drugs. Prejudices based on socioeconomic differences can be almost as strong as those based on race, and nearly every one of her books contains references to differences in life styles and values related to social class. Kerr says her mother sensitized her to such differences.

Ida Meaker "married up," a fact that Kerr says she was proud of in her hometown of Syracuse but defensive about in Auburn. Because Ellis Meaker was a local businessman, Mrs. Meaker was especially concerned that the family not offend the townspeople of Auburn. She would cut the labels from coats and sweaters bought at the big stores in Syracuse lest someone at Second Presbyterian Church interpret their purchases as a lack of support for the hometown merchants. Then she would sew the labels back in prior to visiting her Syracuse relatives. In *Gentlehands*, Kerr uses this kind of self-consciousness about labels to illustrate the contrasting social levels of Skye Pennington and Buddy Boyle.

Mrs. Meaker was too sensitive to describe anyone as "rich." She would either whisper or spell the word much as Mildred does in *I Stay Near You*. Mrs. Meaker also taught Marijane such gems of folk wisdom as the following, all of which have found their way into Kerr's books:

> If you marry a Catholic, there'll be one baby right after the other.
>
> If you marry a boy whose father is bald, he will be bald himself one day.
>
> If you marry an Italian, you won't be allowed to wash the salad bowl; they just wipe them out.
>
> If you marry a mortician, you'll have to do the cosmetic work on the corpses because undertaking is a family business. (SAA, 142)

Kerr treats these not as facts to be learned but as amusing examples of stereotypes that she expects her readers to think about and question.

One of the prejudices that Kerr feels comfortable writing about, probably because she has observed it so closely, is anti-Semitism. There were few Jews in Auburn when the Schwartzes, a childless couple, moved into the Meaker neighborhood. Marijane was surprised at the ripple of adult prejudice that their coming set off. In spite of this, or perhaps because of it, Marijane made friends with the Schwartzes, and their house became her second home. Jews were such strangers to the area that Marijane's father was not sure that it was polite to say "Jew" and instructed Marijane to refer to the Schwartzes as being "of the Jewish persuasion" (*ME*, 14).

In *If I Love You, Am I Trapped Forever?* Alan's grandfather teaches him to use this quaint phraseology, which elicits giggles from other characters as well as from readers. Once a year in Cayuta, Rabbi Goldman gives the Sunday sermon at Second Presbyterian Church, and once a year Reverend Gosnell addresses the Saturday congregation at Temple Emmanuel. Nevertheless, Jews are not numbered among the members of the Cayuta North Country Club even though they control the Yacht Club, and "no one's exactly pushing for intermarriage . . ." (*Trapped,* 2–3). Kerr's point is that prejudice is not limited to the seamier sides of life.

According to *ME ME ME ME ME*, much of the real-life inspiration for the fictional Doomed in *If I Love You . . .* came from Hyman Ginzburg, a Jewish refugee from Nazi Germany who moved to Auburn when he was almost 18. Besides speaking three languages, he wore old-fashioned, gold-rimmed glasses, collected stamps, and played both the violin and the piano. Being 6'4" inches tall, he "made everything all the worse for himself by refusing . . . to go out for basketball" (*ME*, 14).

In *Night Kites*, when Erick asks Nicki whatever happened to Ski (her previous boyfriend), she says, "He was busted for dealing. If your name's Walter Ruski, you get sent up when you break the law. If your name's Richard Gaelen, somebody throws your wife a Bill Ball to get her out of debt" (*Kites*, 61). The reference is to a benefit dance that Erick's mother had given for her best friend Liz Gaelen. Everyone who came had to reach in a fish bowl and pull out a bill and pay it to keep the Gaelens from declaring bankruptcy after Mr. Gaelen was indicted for a Wall Street swindle—a rap he managed to beat.

In *Little Little*, African American Calpurnia Dove and Little Little are in the same English class and compete as writers. When Miss Grossman reads aloud something that Calpurnia has written, Little Little thinks that Miss Grossman is only being nice to Calpurnia because she is black. But Little Little is mature enough to realize that when something she has written gets read aloud, Calpurnia probably "decides Miss Grossman is only being nice to me because I'm a dwarf . . ." (*Little*, 27).

Little Little longs for company and tells of daydreaming that she is from an all-dwarf family: "mother, father, grandparents, and Cowboy all shrunk to my size, living in a little house locked in against a larger world, laughing at them and cursing them, sharing their tyranny with other La Belles" (*Little*, 31).

When Little Little's grandfather takes her to a convention of dwarfs, she is amazed that "coming into view, coming out of cars and around the sides of cars, falling from the heavens for all I knew, were others like me, redheaded, blond, blue-eyed, brown-eyed, straight, twisted, beautiful, ugly, in-between: a world of me" (*Little*, 35). The first person that Little Little speaks to is the beautiful, 4'1" Eloise Ficklin, who snubs Little Little. Afterward, as Little Little gets acquainted with the others, they explain that Eloise never makes friends with dwarfs who are perfectly formed. She is what is called a repudiator. Although her parents make her come to the conventions, she likes to pretend that she is just short, so she picks out the kids who are not like her at all and then acts as though she is helping them out. "The more you're like her," they explain, "the less she'll like you" (*Little,* 37). When Little Little relates the incident to her grandfather that night, he says:

> Well, you have learned something about prejudice today, Little Little. The person at the top of the ladder doesn't pick on the one way at the bottom. He picks on the one on the rung next to him. The fellow way at the bottom picks on the fellow on the ground. There's always someone to look down on, if looking down on someone is your style. (*Little,* 37–38)

Little Little swears that she will never treat anyone that way, but Grandfather La Belle assures her that "no one looks up all the time. When things get tough people drop their eyes. The crucial thing is to remember to raise them back up before you've lost your direction" (*Little,* 38).

Although it is seldom stated so succinctly, Kerr makes this point over and over again. In *Is That You, Miss Blue?* Kerr uses common stereotypes to illustrate prejudices against handicapped people. She shows how the deaf Agnes and the asthmatic Flanders are isolated and then overprotected. The absurdity of putting them together in an out-of-the-way dormitory with only Miss Blue for companionship may go unnoticed by some readers, but Kerr makes sure no one will miss the ridiculousness of the deaf Agnes being fixed up with a blind date who is actually blind.

In looking back and pondering on why she was so drawn to such stories, Kerr said in her "Books Remembered" piece that part of the credit must go to her father's social consciousness and his talking with her about "the depression, the WPA, the CCC—all that was broadcast on the evening news in the thirties."

> But also there was a restless inner feeling that *I* was some-how different, for all of my advantages . . . that I was out-of-step with my peers, faking my way through many of the tribal rites of the times. I felt like some Kafkaish character with a secret,

who didn't know what the secret really was. ("Remembered," unpaged)

For better or for worse, the young Kerr had a habit of eavesdropping on her mother and her mother's friends as they gossiped about the people of Auburn. One day she overheard a disparaging remark about a female gym teacher probably being queer because she was "right out of *The Well of Loneliness*." Marijane was an avid reader—the kind of bright young kid who without even trying becomes a librarian's pet. She spent whole afternoons at the Auburn public library wandering through the adult and even the "closed" sections where she browsed through hundreds of books. She was 12 years old when she overheard her mother's comment and went looking for Radclyffe Hall's *The Well of Loneliness* (Jonathan Cape, 1928), pulled it off the shelves, and began reading with "my hands shaking and my heart beating, knowing that I had stumbled upon myself" ("Remembered," unpaged).

She did not dare check it out but "read it quickly in one afternoon, and then went back and read it more carefully, piecemeal, day by day." Until she read this story, which, as Kerr acknowledges, "is not viewed as exemplary by either lovers of good literature or homophile activists," Kerr had thought "homosexuality was some sort of weird phenomenon which happened to certain males" and had something to do with cross-dressing.

Kerr found Hall's book "both depressing and reassuring. Depressing because of its dire tone, tragic denouement, and harsh stereotyping of the central character . . . but reassuring to a preteen youngster who believed that she was alone in her attraction for members of the same sex" ("Remembered"). For her generation of lesbians, Kerr says that Hall's book must surely have been "the most widely-read book on the subject . . . and in its own time probably more censored, dog-eared, concealed, and reprinted than any other novel." Some girls' parents gave it to them "as a warning against suspected proclivities. And sometimes, reading it was enough to convince less robust spirits to suppress their feelings and march in step, for despite its brave plea for tolerance, it is not a recommendation of any kind" ("Remembered").

The part that touched Kerr the most in this book that she describes as "my first step toward self-acceptance" was the eloquent plea the protagonist's tutor composed in her mind but never dared to say:

> You're neither unnatural nor abominable, nor mad. You're as much a part of what people call nature as anyone else; only you're unexplained as yet—you've not got your niche in creation. But someday that will come, and meanwhile don't shrink from yourself, but just face yourself calmly and bravely . . . But above all be honorable. Cling to your honor for the sake of those others who share the same burden. For their sakes show the world that people like you and they can be quite as selfless and fine as the rest of mankind. (*Remembered*)

Kerr does not speak so directly—at least not to teenagers—about lesbianism. But still her first Vin Packer book, *Spring Fire*, whose writing she negotiated in that dark tunnel between Grand Central Station and the bright sunlight of Park Avenue, was about lesbianism in a sorority. The topic was also part of the Ann Aldrich books that she wrote during the late 1950s and '60s: *We Walk Alone*, *We Too Must Love*, *Carol in a Thousand Cities*, *We Two Won't Last*, and *Take a Lesbian to Lunch*. *Shockproof Sydney Skate*, her popular 1972 book for adults, was about a boy and his mother both being attracted to the same woman. "All coming-out stories are a continuing process," wrote Kerr as the ending to her short story "We Might As Well All Be Strangers," published in the 1994 collection *Am I Blue? Coming Out from the Silence,* edited by Marion Dane Bauer.[2] In the story a young woman tells her mother that she is a lesbian. Her horrified mother cautions the girl against telling her Jewish grandmother, who, having lived through World War II and lost relatives in the Holocaust, "has had enough *tsuris* in life." "If you want to kill an old woman before her time, tell her" ("Strangers," 26). The young woman, however, has already told her grandmother and knows that, in fact, the grandmother's suffering has given her the empathy that the rest of the family lacks.

In all of Kerr's books she campaigns against prejudice. In 1994, when Roger Sutton interviewed her for the *School Library Journal* cover story honoring her receipt of the Margaret A. Edwards award, she told him how shocked she was to hear young teens in Brooklyn use the word *gay* as a simple pejorative to express their disapproval of or dislike for things totally unrelated to sex or gender, comparable to the way they use "retarded" as an all-purpose negative.

For many teens, the concept of homosexuality has become a metaphor for anything they do not understand and therefore dislike and fear. For Kerr, the process is reversed. She uses more easily understood prejudices as a metaphor for homophobia. For example, with *Little Little*, it is to Kerr's credit that she could write a book about a dwarf that was appreciated by members of the group; nevertheless, dwarfs were not the target audience that Kerr had in mind. She was using their dissimilarity to represent all the ways that more typical teenagers feel different. In reference to the incident in which Eloise Ficklin is labeled a repudiator, surely there are more homosexual than dwarf repudiators. It was the concept rather than the specifics that Kerr wanted to convey.

Kerr's 1993 *The Shuteyes* was written for fifth, sixth, and seventh graders under the pen name of Mary James, now publicly identified as M. E. Kerr. Although there is no overt mention of homosexuality, the book is perhaps her most direct attack on prejudice against gays and lesbians. In this science fiction spoof, a boy, his mother, and their neighbor are taken to the planet Alert, where the inhabitants think that sleeping is unnatural and therefore not to be allowed; those who feel a need to shut their eyes are punished.

Although most readers will interpret the story as a lesson against the folly of prejudice in general, it can also be interpreted more specifically as an allegory on homophobia. The condition of wanting and/or needing to sleep affects one in ten citizens; it breaks up families by striking some members but not others; it is "the worst thing you can be, and the worst name anyone can call

In this early spring photo, Kerr enjoys the beach that figures in so many of her stories about Seaville, a fictionalized version of her own East Hampton.

you" (*Shuteyes,* 39); there is a vague fear that those who associate with the afflicted are in danger of developing the condition themselves; the government is sponsoring research to find the cause of the problem; among the most virulent critics are secret snoozers; psychologists try to counsel or hypnotize offenders into normality; some unreceptive sleepers are institutionalized or banished whereas others join protest groups and flaunt their "deviance"; and, in a policy suggestive of the military's "Don't ask; don't tell" compromise, there is less shame if one's sleeping is kept secret.

Presenting such information in the form of a science fiction spoof makes fascinating reading for thoughtful adults, but few children between the ages of 9 and 12 have enough knowledge to catch onto the comparisons. Kerr did not expect them to but instead was hoping to inoculate her readers against the unquestioning acceptance of whatever prejudices they happen to meet.

A second way that Kerr has worked against homophobia is by sprinkling throughout her books direct references to homosexuality, usually in the form of a joke or a snide remark. Some of her mentions are so brief and so nonjudgmental that a quick reading might leave the impression she was teaching prejudice rather than fighting against it, similar to the way that some critics feared that the Archie Bunker character in television's *All in the Family* introduced prejudices to young viewers who lacked the sophistication to realize he was pointing a laughing finger at bigotry.

Superficially the plot of her 1974 *The Son of Someone Famous* centers around Brenda Belle and Adam's sort-of romance, with the two leads taking turns at narrating. Early on, Brenda introduces herself as being 15, "the town tomboy, fatherless, flat-chested, and an only child." She is worried that she is changing into a boy because telephone operators have begun saying things like "Yes, sir," and "Just one moment, sir," and instead of growing breasts she is growing "a small fringe of hair" on her upper lip. Brenda goes into Corps Drugs to buy a depilatory, but she has to hang around for a couple of hours until all the other kids leave. Brenda wants privacy for her transaction, especially from the town's "Most Beautiful," "Most Popular," and "Most Likely to Succeed" Christine Cutler. Brenda has a crush on Christine, which not only makes her "want to puke" but makes her detest herself. "I had decided there was probably something grossly wrong with me, and as a result I had developed a little hunched-over walk, as though I'd be less conspicuous instead of really kinky going around that way" (*Famous,* 5). When Brenda thinks she is finally alone with the druggist, she asks him for "something called Hairgo" and is horribly embarrassed to discover that Adam, the new boy in town, is sitting in the back booth and overhears her request. He joins in the conversation with some clever witticisms, which set the foundation for a friendship that Brenda's mother hopes is a romance but really is not. By the end of the book, readers learn that he too has a crush on Christine Cutler.

Little Little's sister, Cowboy, with her Japanese boyfriend is in some ways similar to Brenda Belle. Little Little explains that her grandfather "has trouble dealing with Cowboy" because "she is too androgynous for him. She has overstayed her time in the tomboy stage" (*Little,* 94). Because Little Little has a hard time making friends and hates to go to other kids' houses where everything is the wrong size, her social life revolves around her specially equipped car. She carefully picks those she invites to ride with her, one of whom is "Gerald Percy, the town sissy," who has to dart "past the jocks who call him 'fag.' "

In *Is That You, Miss Blue?* Kerr writes about the girls at school playing kissing games in their dormitory rooms. Later, she writes about the same subject in a *ME ME ME ME ME* chapter: "There's Not a Man in This Damn Nunnery," where she tells how she and Jan Fox, the most sophisticated person she had ever met in her entire life, would pretend to be Billy and APE (Anna P. Ettinger), the married director and headmistress:

> I'd bend down and kiss Jan, and she'd always think of something "tawdry" to do—slurp my face with her tongue, bite my lip, flick her tongue up in my nostril. I'd draw back and say, "Bee-ly! Bee-ly! Bee-*lee*! How taw-dree!"
> Then we'd collapse laughing. (*ME,* 104)

Two Stuart Hall teachers were lesbians who went everywhere together.

> They looked the way you'd always think lesbians would look: one more masculine, almost totally male-looking until you saw the skirt, stockings, and oxfords . . . the other very feminine. The masculine one was always telling us, "Push yourself!" . . . The feminine one, a very southern lady, easily rattled, was always crying out, "I'm just sick in bed about this, girls." (*ME,* 104)

Jan, Marijane, and Agnes also played "games of being these two teachers kissing, one of us mooning at the other, 'I am sick in bed about you, darling,' while the other embraced her saying, 'Push yourself!' " (*ME,* 105) These sexy games make the three girls feel like such a "wonderful, witty, fast, tight triumvirate" that Marijane forgets to invent a medical excuse for leaving school early.

The next year when Marijane is expelled for buying a dartboard and decorating it with yearbook pictures and disrespectful names of the faculty members, she is surprised at how understanding and supportive her family is. Actually, her mother is relieved because the suspension comes four days prior to the opening of the school play, *The Importance of Being Earnest* by Oscar Wilde. For weeks, Marijane had been practicing the part of Algernon Moncrieff, and Mrs. Meaker did not want her daughter dressing in nineteenth-century drag, no matter how literary the purpose.

In *Love Is a Missing Person,* Suzy Slade feels especially sad when a gang of girls shave her sister's head because she had just told Suzy that she is growing her hair out to become more feminine and was even thinking of taking back her real name of Priscilla (*Missing,* 150). Earlier, Suzy had described Chicago as "my crazy sister in drag" (*Missing,* 51).

At the beginning of *If I Love You, Am I Trapped Forever?* Alan says:

> The thing is: I'm not going to describe in detail the very personal things that take place between me and Leah. I'm not writing this book for a bunch of voyeurs. I'm tired of books written for voyeurs. Go out and get your own experience, any of you voyeurs who happen to be reading this. It's a story about people and how their minds work, not a story about how their bodies work. (*Trapped,* 13–14)

Critic Robert Unsworth, writing in *School Library Journal,* [3] conjectured that it was not voyeurs but censors that Kerr was avoiding. A more likely explanation is that Kerr sincerely wants her readers to ponder the differences between physical and intellectual love, a point she later develops more fully in her short story "Do You Want My Opinion?" (see chapter 5).

As the years went by, Kerr's casual references to homosexuality became more fully developed. In *Fell Down* she wrote about the friendship between Lenny and Nels:

> Of the pair, it was Nels who could express affection, and Lenny who didn't know how.
>
> Lenny wished he could be more relaxed and accepting.
>
> Instead, he would cringe down the school hall when Nels called out, "Hey, Lover-Boy, wait up!"
>
> He would jump when Nels took his arm under an umbrella.
>
> He would suffer, get red, and then ask Nels, "What's this thing you have about acting like a fairy when people are watching us?"
>
> "A fairy wouldn't dare act as I do, Lenny."
>
> "I guess not. . . ." (*Fell Down*, 49)

"Nels had a nickname for Lenny too, but Lenny loathed being called it. Tra La. From Tralatski" (*Fell Down*, 63). When the two boys are having an argument, Nels says,

> "I swear I don't remember you telling me that. Don't be mad at Nell, okay?"
>
> "Do you have to call yourself that?" Lenny asked him.
>
> "My father was called that and his father was, too. It's a proud old name in our family."
>
> "It sounds faggy."
>
> "Not to us. . . ." (*Fell Down*, 61)

Later in the story when Fell is trying to find out what happened to Nels Plummer, he goes to talk to the boy who now has the dummy. The boy gets

> off a few remarks about Sevens that were more obscene than they were anything else. And naturally he said we were all faggots because it always comes down to that with Neanderthal types. (*Fell Down*, 92)

In her 1994 *Frankenlouse*, Nick's Dad is worried that 17-year-old Aaron Bindle is taking the 12-year-old daughter of a movie star to the Halloween Ball.

"I didn't know an upperclassman would date a worm [a beginning student]," said my father.

"Probably he wouldn't before this year, sir," I said, "since that would have made him gay." It was our first year with females enrolled.

"We don't say gay," my father said. "Gay means elated. We say homosexual."

"*They* say, gay, sir."

"We don't. We say homosexual," said my father. (*Frankenlouse*, 69)

In *I'll Love You When You're More Like Me*, Wally's best friend is Charlie Gilhooley, who, when he was 16, began telling a few close associates that "he believed he preferred boys to girls." This should not have been news to people who knew Charlie, "but honesty had its own rewards: ostracism and disgrace" (*Like Me*, 38). In another place, Charlie complains "You can make straight *A*'s and *A*+'s for ten years of school, and on one afternoon, in a weak moment, confess you think you're gay. What do you think you'll be remembered as thereafter? Not the straight *A* student." Wally's dad "has an assortment of names for Charlie: limp wrist; weak sister; flying saucer; fruitstand; thweetheart; fairy tale; cupcake, on and on," but he never uses those names to Charlie's face because "After all, everybody's going to die someday, including the Gilhooleys; why make their only son uncomfortable and throw business to Annan Funeral Home?" (*Like Me*, 40). An older Charlie makes a cameo appearance in *Night Kites* where he wanders into the plot by entering the Kingdom by the Sea bar and getting both of his arms broken by the homophobic bouncer who fears that, once gays start coming to a bar, it will be the end of all "regular" business.

Night Kites is as much about homosexuality and a family's adjustment to the fact that one of their children is homosexual as is *Deliver Us from Evie*. However, it was not perceived as a personal statement in the same way that *Evie* was. One reason is that the protagonist was male, so people were less inclined to look for autobiographical elements; another is that the AIDS aspect of the story made people interpret it as a book about confronting death rather than a book about confronting life. Also, shortly after *Deliver Us from Evie* came out, Kerr published her short story "We Might As Well All Be Strangers," contributed her "Books Remembered" piece to the Children's Book Council, and wrote the introduction to Roger Sutton's *Hearing Us Out: Voices from the Gay and Lesbian Community*.[4] She said this introduction to *Hearing Us Out* was the coming-out piece she always meant to write but that nobody ever asked for.

One of the chief values of both *Night Kites* and *Deliver Us from Evie* is the way they discuss stereotypes and illustrate that homosexuals are individuals; some fit cultural expectations and some do not. When read in tandem, the two books illustrate a paradigm or a set of stages experienced in some degree by most families in which a young person is gay. As illustrated below, there is first a period of curiosity followed by various kinds of denial and attempts to fix blame. In these stages, most families experience instances, if not intervals, of frustration and fear that usually lead to the beginning of acceptance, at least by some family members.

Curiosity

The young person who suspects that he or she is unusual in being attracted to others of the same sex will be especially alert to the kinds of references that Kerr drops into her books and what they reveal about family and social attitudes. In *Night Kites*, big brother Pete tells Erick that during high school he "became the world's foremost authority on gay books. . . . Migod! I don't think there's a book that even remotely touched on the subject that I didn't read. I spent hours in the library looking under H in the card catalog!" (*Kites,* 107).

In *Night Kites* the curiosity stage is also illustrated through Mrs. Rudd's actions the previous summer when Pete had told her he was gay. In what might be either wish fulfillment or the modeling of behavior Kerr would like parents to follow, Mrs. Rudd does not overreact nor does she share the news with others.

Instead, she begins reading about homosexuality and pondering its implications.

In *Deliver Us from Evie*, Evie drops hints—as when she argues with her mother—to make her family think about the matter: "Some people like me the way I am," and her mother says, "But you don't like *him*." "I'm not talking about Cord Whittle!" says Evie. After her mother goes to bed, Evie reads a poem to Parr that, in spite of its ambiguity, is clearly a love poem to Patsy. Evie says, no, "It's all in the imagination. . . . It's not about anyone." Parr concludes that she must have been bombed or she would not have read it to him, or "maybe something was going on with her that was just bursting to come out" (*Evie,* 25).

While pondering what is happening Parr remembers:

> Dad had a distant cousin who farmed in Quincy, Illinois. Cousin Joe. Dad called him Cousin Josephine because he'd lived on a farm with another old man for thirty years. They were a couple, Dad said—"a couple of fruits." I remember Dad watching their pickup come down our road on a visit once telling Mom, "Cousin Josephine's here with his wife," then laughing, and ducking Mom's palm as she tried to swipe him. (*Evie,* 37)

Later as Parr wonders about his mother's statement that homosexuality is a sin, he asks Cord, "Do you think being a dyke is sinful?" "*Hell* no!" responds Cord. "It's not serious enough to be a sin. It's kid stuff. Two women is . . . Now two men—that's another matter. That's sin in the Bible" (*Evie,* 101).

Denial

Cord not only believes that lesbianism is "kid stuff"; he thinks it is just a stage. Cord likes Evie, even loves her, and tells Parr that although "Evie's what I'd choose for my wife, Patsy's another story. I'd like to *change* that little gal." Parr tells him he is asking for an early grave; "Duff would kill you with his bare hands." Cord laughingly agrees, "But I can dream, can't I, Parr?" (*Evie,* 102).

When Parr hints that it is almost as unlikely that Evie will ever become his wife, Cord says "Clothes do not make the man." Laughing at his witticism, he goes on "She's still Evie. We just got to get her past this stage she's in" (*Evie,* 103). The same motif appears in *Night Kites* when Nicki laughingly claims that if she could get her hands on Charlie Gilhooley she could change him.

It is not just family and friends but also young homosexuals who practice denial. Although Evie appears confident in identifying herself as a lesbian, this confidence did not come until she met someone else like herself. Evie's mother says,

> I'm not going to get into an argument with you, Evie. I'm going to tell you what I think. If this is *true*, if you really are what you say you are, all the more reason for trying to fix yourself up a little. Be more presentable. Be a little more feminine. (*Evie,* 85)

Evie's answer is that Patsy likes her the way she is, with her hair slicked back, dressed in her brother's bomber jacket, putting her hands in her pockets and taking long steps. "The only thing she didn't like was my smoking. The only reason she didn't like my smoking was because it isn't good for my health. So I gave it up!" (*Evie,* 86). In *Night Kites*, when Peter is trying to explain to Erick why he never shared the fact that he was gay, he says "I thought you sort of knew anyway." "How would I sort of know?" I said. "You sort of know about someone like Charlie Gilhooley, but how would I sort of know about you?"

Pete confesses that he always stayed as far away as possible from Charlie:

> "Sometimes, when I was a kid, *I* felt like beating him up. I'd tell myself I might be gay, but I'm not a Charlie Gilhooley fairy!"
> "Well, you're not," Erick says and Pete responds, "So what? . . . Do I get extra points for not looking it? . . . I used to think I did." (*Kites,* 94)

Although Kerr's intention with this scene was to acknowledge the existence of attitudes like Pete's and to deal with them, it is nevertheless disturbing to some gays. Pete changed his mind when he met a "political gay" who convinced him that, yes, it was his own private business what he did in bed, "but what about life out of bed? What about lying to everyone, trying to pass for straight, never letting family or friends know what was going on . . . ?" Peter decided that "the only way to get past that kind of self-hatred was to come out of hiding" (*Kites*, 95), and so the previous summer he had told their mother and planned on telling Erick next, but then he got sick.

Blame

Three kinds of blame are involved. One is to resent and blame the young person's partner. When Evie's mother is talking with Parr, she blames Patsy Duff for starting "this thing" and laments that, if it is true that Evie is a lesbian, it is going to be much harder for her than for the attractive (i.e., the feminine looking) Patsy Duff. Unlike Patsy, Evie "can't pass herself off as something else. It isn't in her nature." Then Mrs. Burrman adds, "I just hope Evie has the name without the game. It's bad enough to look that way, but it's awful to look it and actually be it. . . . Then you're a stereotype. You're what everybody's always thought one of those women was like." Parr counters that he is a stereotypical farm boy. "I'm driving around on tractors, going to 4-H, planting in the spring, harvesting in the fall—what's the difference?" "The difference," says his mother "is you're not against the law, Parr. And the church doesn't call you a sinner" (*Evie*, 66–67).

In *Night Kites* even though the family has learned that Pete has been gay ever since high school and has had dozens of partners, they are so resentful and critical of his present partner Jim that the sympathetic Erick observes "Jim's in a no-win situation here" (*Kites*, 162). The more pervasive blame that usually causes more grief relates to people trying to figure out why someone is homo-sexual. Evie's mother suggests that Patsy is a lesbian because of her mother's alcoholism, which Evie hotly denies and asks "Do you think I'm the way I am because of something you and Dad did?" Her mother answers:

> I don't think it helped that your father got you all interested in repairing tractors and doing other male things. Just because Doug wasn't good at that kind of work didn't mean you had to take it on. (*Evie,* 113)

Evie responds, "Oh, Mom, get real. I came out of the womb ready to handle tools. . . . You couldn't have learned it if Dad had spent an hour every day of the week instructing you!" (*Evie,* 113). This statement is the kind that causes some critics to accuse Kerr of promoting stereotypes. "Is there really a correlation," they ask, "between how well one handles tools and being either straight or gay?"

In *Night Kites*, Mr. Rudd says that maybe if they had paid more attention to Pete when he was Erick's age, "we wouldn't be in this situation!"

> Mom said, "Now listen to me. I've had a whole summer to think about this. I read about it, too. This is not something that's our fault."
> "I'm not talking about *our* fault," Dad jumped in immediately.
> "What *are* you talking about, Arthur?"
> "The only way Pete runs true to type is that he's always been a mamma's boy! Half the time while Pete was growing up, you two were off in a corner talking French together, giggling, carrying on!" (*Kites,* 134)

As the argument progresses, Mrs. Rudd says to Erick in reference to Mr. Rudd, "Don't bother to explain anything to him," and Mr. Rudd answers "That's right! Keep me in the dark, where I've been all the while *you* raised the family!" (*Kites,* 134–35).

The third kind of blame is the association of tragedy with homosexuality. The idea that having AIDS is punishment for Pete's behavior runs just below the surface all through *Night Kites*. In *Deliver Us from Evie* it is shown through Parr's last conversation with Angel Kidder when they run into each other at the Salvation Army aid center in Duffton after the flood has forced both families out of their homes. In response to Parr's "Can we talk?" Angel begins with "Maybe it's God using the river. Daddy says maybe this is to teach us something" (*Evie,* 169). The first night of the rainstorm, Parr had been late in getting Angel home because Angel had begged to stay parked out behind the school gymnasium just a little bit longer, but now she says it was Parr's fault, "I wasn't the one in charge, or driving the car. Maybe I didn't know better, but *you* should have. You're the boy." Parr doesn't know how to respond, especially when she goes on:

> "Of course, who's the boy and who's the girl is all mixed up in some people's thinking. Some people think there's no difference, and I guess I got to thinking all kinds of crazy things myself, since I was actually cheering on your sister and Patsy Duff. I remember *that*. That was my own faulty thinking."
>
> I put my hand on her shoulder. "Angel, you don't even sound like yourself. I know this has been awful, but don't start blaming it on things like Evie and Patsy and sin and bad thoughts. If you live in Florida, you get hit by a hurricane. If you live in California, it's an earthquake does you in. Here, it's the rivers. It's geography, not morality." (*Evie,* 170)

As Angel disagrees with Parr's assertion that "I just don't think it's right to blame this flood on God. All these people aren't sinners," she says, "I'm not the only one saying it, Parr. A lot of people are asking, How come this happened?" (*Evie,* 171).

Frustration and Fear

In both books, there is enough frustration and fear to be shared by all. In *Night Kites*, Erick's father is terribly upset when he comes home and finds Erick and his friend Jack in a situation that makes it appear that they are lovers. Even after the confusion is straightened out, Erick is so sensitive about sticking to his masculine role that when he uses his mother's hair dryer he turns on the bathtub water so no one will hear.

Pete reassures Erick that when he gets out of college he will not be like Pete was in wanting "to dance and drink and play."

> No. You're having your party right now. My adolescence was on hold. . . . I could hardly take Tim Lathrop to the Seaville High Prom, or Marty to the P-Party. We sneaked around like guilty thieves. Tim spent half his time at confession, and Marty was seeing if a shrink could make him straight. (*Kites,* 96–97)

Even when Pete's family is trying to be accepting of Pete's friend Jim, they do not know how. But neither does Pete. He confesses to Erick that he feels no love for Jim and in fact cannot even use the word. He suspects that Jim does not love him either but is reluctant to walk out on him now that he has AIDS. If it had not been for Pete's illness, "We'd have just been good buddies after we came back from Europe" (*Kites,* 177). Erick thinks that Pete is misjudging Jim and wonders if their dad is right, that Pete's a quitter who never sees anything through.

Pete says he has always had a problem being openly gay and talking with straights about his gay feelings.

> I think relationships scared the hell out of me. I guess it was because if one lasted, I'd have to face a lot of shit I didn't want to. I'd be seen with one guy all the time. How could I explain that to the family, and straight friends, and people from Southworth [the private school where he teaches]? . . . I'm not saying that I deliberately set out to sabotage every relationship I ever had, but I think a lot of those feelings were in operation. . . . So I never stayed with anyone very long. (*Kites,* 179)

The difference in the way families treat romances between opposite and same-sex partners is clearly shown in both books. In *Night Kites*, Erick's family is all for his dating nice-girl Dill. And although he keeps his sexual exploits with wild-girl Nicki secret, it is hard to imagine that, if they found out, they would have been other than relieved. After all, one of Mr. Rudd's regular bits of advice to his sons is to "sow their wild oats" while they are young so when they marry they can settle down.

The clearer example occurs in *Evie*, when the Burrmans celebrate Valentine's Day. They make a big fuss about it mainly because winter on the farm is so long and boring. Evie is going to drive over and pick up Angel, who is coming to dinner. Even Mr. Burrman is in a party mood, having bought a big box of chocolates and a mushy "To my wife" card. Parr has made a valentine for Angel and bought her a locket, which he hopes his mother will wrap for him. She happily agrees and dashes into Evie's room looking for a scissors. She notices on the bed an opened package addressed to Jane Doe. Evie comes back from her shower to confront her mother's questions. She "confesses" to having received a Valentine's gift from Patsy and to having a post office box in King's Corners through which she and Patsy have been corresponding. In an ugly scene, Evie bemoans that she is 18 years old and still has to sneak around.

Acceptance

Many families never come to a full acceptance of their child's homosexuality, but in Kerr's stories they come to partial acceptance at least. An early step is for the family to feel defensive and to rally against outside criticism. They begin to accept the homosexuality not as a family trait but as an oddity—something that just happened. In reference to his dad's cousin and his gay partner, Parr says,

> I never thought much about them, and when the thing with Evie and Patsy started, I didn't think they were the same way. Evie was just impressed by Patsy Duff, and I knew by then the feeling was mutual. I didn't take it beyond the point. I wasn't sure Mom had even got that far yet. (*Evie*, 37–38)

When Mrs. Burrman laments that if Evie is a lesbian, life is going to be hard for her, Parr shudders at the harsh sound of the word "lesbian," but "It was a relief to tell the truth: to admit that my sister's way wasn't going to be fixed by a turtleneck sweater or a skirt. She was deep-down different" (*Evie*, 66).

After she learns that Evie gave up smoking because of Patsy, Mrs. Burrman begins to understand that Patsy's influence may not be all bad. Even Mr. Burrman comes to Evie's defense when, following Cord's sign campaign, Sheriff Starr says that at Mr. Duff's request, he has come to warn Evie to stay away from Patsy. " 'Warn *her* to stay away from Evie!' Dad barked." Evie's response to the sheriff is "Far as I know, there's no law against two females seeing each other." The sheriff has to agree that he has never heard of one either, but he is just doing his duty. Then he says about the sign, "I don't know if there's truth to it or not, but even if there is—" Mrs. Burrman jumps in with "Even if there is, *what?*" When the sheriff says that "Patsy Duff *is* a minor," Mr. Burrman says,

> "Yes, she is, but Evie's not selling Patsy Duff liquor or trying to marry her"—he gave a snort—"or registering her to vote. I mean, *what* law is Evie breaking that I'm supposed to do something about?" (*Evie,* 129)

As Mrs. Burrman becomes tearful, the sheriff tries to be consoling:

> "I'll tell you something. I don't even think this thing is important. I had an uncle who was funny, and you wouldn't meet a nicer fellow. He didn't bother anyone, and—"
> "Evie's not *funny,*" said my mother. "She's not some freak."
> "Neither was my uncle Bob. . . . I didn't meant he was a freak. He was more a fluke. All families got a fluke—if not right in front of them, way back. We even had a rooster out to our place once you couldn't get to go near the hens for love or money! It happens!" (*Evie,* 129–30)

Mrs. Burrman asks Sheriff Starr if he told all this to Mr. Duff. He responds "Did you ever try to tell Duffy anything?" He then explains that Patsy has always been a rebel; she is the one thing Duffy cannot control. "That's what this is all about. She's going through a stage." " 'And Evie?' Mom asked. He shrugged and grinned. 'Evie's what she is, and whatever that is, it hasn't bothered anyone before, has it?' " (*Evie,* 130)

Kerr said she purposely gave no sign of Mr. Duff's softening in his attitude because in real life there are families, or at least family members, who never accept the homosexuality of a child.

When Kerr was questioned about her reaction to this outlining of the events in her two books, she laughingly protested that a young person's being gay was not quite an Alfred Lord Tennyson and Arthur Hallam kind of tragedy—not something to be mourned for 30 years.

Although it is true that homosexuality is not a tragedy, the alienation of families is. A survey by the National Gay and Lesbian Task Force reported that one in four gay teens leaves home because of conflicts with their parents about sexual identity.[5] Although being accepted by one's family is not the only challenge faced by gays and lesbians, for teenagers it may be the most pressing. And it may be one that appropriate literature can help.

In the foreword to *Hearing Us Out,* Kerr wrote that her father, the man she had been so close to all through her childhood, was never able to bring himself to speak with her about her sexual orientation. Her mother spoke about it perhaps too much, saying such things as "I hate that word *lesbian* and I'll never call you one!", don't "bring any of them to this house!", and "stay in New York City where anything goes, because around here I couldn't hold my head up if it ever got out." Kerr laments that her parents "so in thrall to convention and conformity . . . missed the chance to know my warm and loving friends—as well as to know me better." She wrote that Sutton's collection of interviews made her think of

> what this book might have meant not just to someone like me, growing up gay, but also to a parent like my mother, who was not that different from many of her time. If only there had been literature for her to read, besides the heavy and pathetic *Well of Loneliness*. If only she had some confirmation that this blight on our family was not as rare and terrible as she believed it was. (*Out*, foreword)

Thanks to both nonfiction and fiction writers, today's generation of curious young readers—along with their siblings and their parents—are able to go to bookstores and libraries and openly select books that answer questions about physical and emotional aspects of homosexuality. These publications also tell intriguing stories about what it means to be different from the majority, whether through sexual orientation, ethnic identification, socio-economic status, physical condition, or intellectual ability. M. E. Kerr deserves a goodly portion of the credit for this happier state of affairs.

Notes and References

Unless otherwise noted, page numbers for Kerr's novels and short stories refer to those in the original hardback copies.

Chapter 1

1. M. E. Kerr, *ME ME ME ME ME: Not a Novel* (New York: HarperCollins, 1983); hereafter cited as *ME*.

2. *Something About the Author Autobiography Series 1* (Detroit: Gale, 1986), 141–54; hereafter cited as SAA.

Chapter 2

1. Laura Winston, "Devotedly, Patrick Henry Casebolt," *Ladies Home Journal* (September 1951).

2. M. E. Kerr, *Dinky Hocker Shoots Smack!* (New York: Harper-Collins, 1972), 46; Dell Laurel Leaf paperback, seventh printing, 1977; hereafter cited as *Dinky*.

3. Roger Sutton, "A Conversation with M. E. Kerr," *School Library Journal* (June 1993): 27; hereafter cited as Sutton.

4. Mary Kingsbury, "The Why of People: The Novels of M. E. Kerr," *Horn Book Magazine* (June 1977): 188–95.

5. M. E. Kerr, *Little Little* (New York: HarperCollins, 1981), 183; hereafter cited as *Little*.

6. M. E. Kerr, "The People Behind the Books: On Cover Art II," in *Literature for Today's Young Adults,* 4th edition. Alleen Pace Nilsen and Kenneth L. Donelson (New York: HarperCollins, 1993), 436.

Chapter 3

1. M. E. Kerr, *Gentlehands* (New York: HarperCollins, 1978), 2; hereafter cited as *Gentlehands*.

2. Ruth Charnes, *Interracial Books for Children Bulletin* 9:8 (1978): 18.

3. Arthea Reed, *The ALAN Review* 11:1 (Fall, 1983): 29.

4.   Nancy Hammond, *Horn Book Magazine* (December, 1983): 462.

5.   M. E. Kerr, *Night Kites* (New York: HarperCollins, 1986), 12; hereafter cited as *Kites*.

6.   Claudia Morrow, *School Library Journal* (November, 1994): 121.

7.   M. E. Kerr, *Deliver Us from Evie* (New York: HarperCollins, 1994), 1; hereafter cited as *Evie*.

Chapter 4

1.   Jim Roginsky, "M. E. Kerr: An Interview," *The ALAN Review* 16:1 (Fall 1988): 40; hereafter cited as Roginsky.

2.   M. E. Kerr, *If I Love You, Am I Trapped Forever?* (New York: HarperCollins, 1973), 2; hereafter cited as *Trapped*.

3.   Mary Burns, *Horn Book Magazine* (August 1975): 385.

4.   M. E. Kerr, *Is That You, Miss Blue?* (New York: HarperCollins, 1975), 7; hereafter cited as *Blue*.

5.   M. E. Kerr, "Feed the Wonder," *The ALAN Review* 10:1 (Fall, 1982): 1–2.

6.   Mrs. John G. Gray, "Young People's Books," *Best Sellers* (May 1975): 49.

7.   Lillian Gerhardt, *School Library Journal* (November 1975): 176.

8.   M. E. Kerr, *Love Is a Missing Person* (New York: HarperCollins, 1975), 132; hereafter cited as *Missing*.

9.   M. E. Kerr, *I'll Love You When You're More Like Me* (New York: HarperCollins, 1977), 182–83; hereafter cited as *Like Me*.

10.   M. E. Kerr, *What I Really Think of You* (New York: Harper-Collins, 1982), 29; hereafter cited as *Think*.

11.   M. E. Kerr, *Him She Loves?* (New York: HarperCollins, 1984), 4; hereafter cited as *Him*.

12.   M. E. Kerr, *Fell* (New York: HarperCollins, 1987), 5; hereafter cited as *Fell*.

13.   Marjorie Lewis, *School Library Journal* (September, 1989): 272.

14.   M. E. Kerr, *Fell Down* (New York: HarperCollins, 1991): 12; hereafter cited as *Fell Down*.

15.   M. E. Kerr, *Linger* (New York: HarperCollins, 1993), 7–8; hereafter cited as *Linger*.

16.   Patricia Manning, *School Library Journal* (June, 1990): 124.

17.   Mary James, *Shoebag* (New York: Scholastic Apple, 1990), 49; hereafter cited as *Shoebag*.

18.   Mary James, *The Shuteyes* (New York: Scholastic, 1993), 63; hereafter cited as *Shuteyes*.

19.   Ruth Vose, *School Library Journal* (April, 1993): 120.

20.   Mary James, *Frankenlouse* (New York: Scholastic, 1994), 10; hereafter cited as *Frankenlouse*.

Chapter 5

1. M. E. Kerr, *The Son of Someone Famous* (New York: Harper-Collins, 1974), 10; hereafter cited as *Famous.*

2. M. E. Kerr, "The People Behind the Books," in *Literature for Today's Young Adults,* 2d ed. Alleen Pace Nilsen and Kenneth L. Donelson (Glenview, Illinois: Scott-Foresman, 1985), 341.

3. M. E. Kerr, "The Sweet Perfume of Good-Bye," in *Visions: Nineteen Short Stories by Outstanding Writers for Young Adults,* ed. Donald R. Gallo (New York: Dell Laurel Leaf, 1988), 186–90; hereafter cited as *Perfume.*

4. M. E. Kerr, "Sunny Days and Sunny Nights," in *Connections: Short Stories by Outstanding Writers for Young Adults,* ed. Donald R. Gallo (New York: Delacorte, 1989), 218–26; hereafter cited as *Sunny.*

5. M. E. Kerr, "Do You Want My Opinion?" in *Sixteen: Short Stories by Outstanding Writers for Young Adults,* ed. Donald R. Gallo (New York: Dell Laurel Leaf, 1984), 93–98; hereafter cited as *Opinion.*

6. Mary James, *Shoebag Returns.* Read in manuscript prior to publication by Scholastic 1996.

Chapter 6

1. M. E. Kerr, *Fell Back* (New York: HarperCollins, 1989), 59; hereafter cited as *Fell Back.*

Chapter 7

1. Lawrence Mintz, oral presentation at Fifth International Conference on Humor, Cork, Ireland, June 1985.

Chapter 8

1. M. E. Kerr, "Books Remembered," *Children's Book Council Features* 48:2 (Fall-Winter, 1995): unpaged; hereafter cited as "Remembered."

2. M. E. Kerr, "We Might As Well All Be Strangers," in *Am I Blue? Coming Out from the Silence,* ed. Marion Dane Bauer (New York: HarperCollins, 1994), 21–26; hereafter cited as *Strangers.*

3. Robert Unsworth, "Holden Caulfield, Where Are You?" *School Library Journal* (January 1977): 40–41.

4. M. E. Kerr, "Foreword," *Hearing Us Out: Voices from the Gay and Lesbian Community,* by Roger Sutton (New York: Little Brown, 1994); hereafter cited as *Out.*

5. Roger Sutton, *Hearing Us Out: Voices from the Gay and Lesbian Community* (New York: Little Brown, 1994), 11.

Appendix:
Honors and Prizes Won
by M. E. Kerr

Dinky Hocker Shoots Smack!

Best of the Best Books (YA) 1970–1983, ALA
Best Children's Books of 1972, *School Library Journal*
ALA Notable Children's Books of 1972
Cited for Margaret A. Edwards Award, 1993

If I Love You, Am I Trapped Forever?

Honor Book, *Book World* Children's Spring Book Festival, 1973
Outstanding Children's Books of 1973, *The New York Times*

The Son of Someone Famous

Best Children's Books of 1975, *School Library Journal*
"Best of the Best" 1966–1978, *School Library Journal*

Is That You, Miss Blue?

Outstanding Children's Books of 1975, *The New York Times*
ALA Notable Children's Books of 1975
Best Books for Young Adults, 1975, ALA

Gentlehands

Best of the Best Books 1966–1992, ALA
Best Books for Young Adults, 1978, ALA
ALA Notable Children's Books of 1978
Best Children's Books of 1978, *School Library Journal*
Winner, 1978 Christopher Award

Best Children's Books of 1978, *The New York Times*
Cited for Margaret A. Edwards Award, 1993

Little Little

ALA Notable Children's Books of 1981
Best Books for Young Adults, 1981, ALA
Best Books of 1981, *School Library Journal*
Winner, 1981 Golden Kite Award, Society of Children's Book Writers

What I Really Think of You

Best Books of 1982, *School Library Journal*

ME ME ME ME ME: *Not a Novel*

Best Books for Young Adults, 1983
Cited for Margaret A. Edwards Award, 1993

I Stay Near You

Best Books for Young Adults, 1985

Night Kites

Best of the Best Books 1966–1980, ALA
Best Books for Young Adults, 1986, ALA
Booklist Best of the '80s
Recommended Books for Reluctant YA Readers, 1987, ALA
1992 California Young Reader Award
Cited for Margaret A. Edwards Award, 1993

Fell

Best Books for Young Adults, 1987, ALA
Booklist Editors' Choice, 1987

Fell Back

Finalist, 1990 Edgar Allan Poe Award, Best Young Adult Mystery (Mystery Writers of America)

Deliver Us from Evie

Best Books for Young Adults, 1995, ALA

Booklist Editors' Choice, 1994
Recommended Books for Reluctant Young Adult Readers, 1995, ALA
Horn Book Fanfare Honor List, 1995
School Library Journal's Best Books, 1994
1994 Best Book Honor Award, Michigan Library Association

Selected Bibliography

Primary Sources

Novels

Deliver Us from Evie. New York: HarperCollins, 1994.
Dinky Hocker Shoots Smack! New York: HarperCollins, 1972.
Fell. New York: HarperCollins, 1987.
Fell Back. New York: HarperCollins, 1989.
Fell Down. New York: HarperCollins, 1991.
Frankenlouse. (Under Mary James, pseud.) New York: Scholastic, 1994.
Gentlehands. New York: HarperCollins, 1978.
"Hello," I Lied. New York: HarperCollins forthcoming 1997.
Him She Loves? New York: HarperCollins, 1984.
I Stay Near You. New York: HarperCollins, 1985.
If I Love You, Am I Trapped Forever? New York: HarperCollins, 1973.
I'll Love You When You're More Like Me. New York: HarperCollins, 1977.
Is That You, Miss Blue? New York: HarperCollins, 1975.
Linger. New York: HarperCollins, 1993.
Little Little. New York: HarperCollins, 1981.
Love Is a Missing Person. New York: HarperCollins, 1975.
Night Kites. New York: HarperCollins, 1986.
Shoebag. (Under Mary James, pseud.) New York: Scholastic, 1990.
Shoebag Returns. (Under Mary James, pseud.) New York: Scholastic, 1997.
The Shuteyes. (Under Mary James, pseud.) New York: Scholastic, 1993.
The Son of Someone Famous. New York: HarperCollins, 1974.
What I Really Think of You. New York: HarperCollins, 1982.

Nonfiction

Blood on the Forehead. New York: HarperCollins, forthcoming.
Sudden Endings. (Under Vin Packer, pseud.) New York: Doubleday, 1964; Fawcett.

Autobiographical Works

"Books Remembered." *Children's Book Council Features* 48:2 (Fall-Winter, 1995).
"Feed the Wonder." *ALAN Review* (Fall 1982): 1–2.
"Foreword." *Hearing Us Out: Voices from the Gay and Lesbian Community* by Roger Sutton. Boston: Little, Brown, 1994.
Kerr, M. E. "M. E. Kerr." In *Speaking for Ourselves,* comp. and ed. Donald R. Gallo. Urbana, Ill.: National Council of Teachers of English, 1990.
ME ME ME ME ME: Not a Novel. New York: HarperCollins, 1983.
Something about the Author Autobiography Series I: 141–54. Detroit: Gale, 1986.

Short Stories

"The Author." In *Funny You Should Ask: The Delacorte Book of Original Humorous Short Stories,* ed. David Gale. New York: Delacorte, 1992. Also published in *Scope* (26 March 1993).
"Devotedly, Patrick Henry Casebolt." (Under Laura Winston, pseud.) *Ladies' Home Journal* (September 1951).
"Do You Want My Opinion?" In *Sixteen: Short Stories by Outstanding Writers for Young Adults,* ed. Donald R. Gallo. New York: Delacorte, 1984. Also published in *Seventeen* (September 1984).
"The Green Killer." In *Bad Behavior,* ed. Mary Higgins Clark. San Diego: Harcourt Brace, 1995.
"Like Father, Like Son." *Scope* (3 November 1995).
"Son of a One Eye." *Scope* (October 1989).
"Sunny Days and Sunny Nights." In *Connections: Short Stories by Outstanding Writers for Young Adults,* ed. Donald R. Gallo. New York: Delacorte, 1989.
"The Sweet Perfume of Good-bye." In *Visions: Nineteen Short Stories by Outstanding Writers for Young Adults,* ed. Donald R. Gallo. New York: Delacorte, 1988.
"We Might As Well All Be Strangers." In *Am I Blue? Coming Out from the Silence,* ed. Marion Dane Bauer. New York: HarperCollins, 1994.

Secondary Sources

Books

Bryfonski, Dedria, ed. *Contemporary Literary Criticism* 12:296–303. Detroit: Gale, 1980.
Commire, Anne, ed. *Something about the Author* 20:124. Detroit: Gale, 1980.

Nilsen, Alleen P., and Kenneth L. Donelson. *Literature for Today's Young Adults*, 2d ed. Glenview, Ill.: Scott, Foresman, 1985. Also 4th ed. New York: HarperCollins, 1993.

Hipple, Ted. *Writers for Young Adults*. New York: Scribner's, 1996.

Articles and Interviews

DeLuca, Geraldine. "Taking True Risks: Controversial Issues in Young Adult Novels." *The Lion and the Unicorn* 3:2 (Winter, 1979–80): 125–48.

FitzGerald, Jennifer. "Challenging the Pressure to Conform: Byars and Kerr." *School Library Journal* (September 1986): 46–47.

Gray, A. "Her, her, her: An Interview with M. E. Kerr." *Voice of Youth Advocates (VOYA)* (February 1991).

Hartvigsen, M. Kip, and Christen Borg Hartvigsen. "The Terrible Hilarity of Adolescence in *Dinky Hocker Shoots Smack!*" *The ALAN Review* (Fall 1986).

Janeczko, Paul. "An Interview with M. E. Kerr." *English Journal* (December 1975): 75–77.

Kaye, Marilyn "Recurring Patterns in the Novels of M. E. Kerr." *Children's Literature: Annual of the MLA Seminar on Children's Literature by The Children's Literature Association* 7 (1978): 226–32.

Kingsbury, Mary. "The Why of People: The Novels of M. E. Kerr." *Horn Book* (June 1977): 188–95.

Mazer, Norma Fox. "I Love It! It's Your Best Book!" *English Journal* (February 1986): 26–29.

Piehl, Kathy. "The Business of Religion in M. E. Kerr's Novels." *Voice of Youth Advocates (VOYA)* (February 1985): 307–10, 363.

Roginsky, Jim. "M. E. Kerr: An Interview." *The ALAN Review* (Fall 1988): 37–41. Also published in *Behind the Covers: Interviews with Authors and Illustrators of Children's and Young Adult Books* Vol. 2. Englewood, Colo.: Libraries Unlimited, 1989.

Scholastic Fiction. "Mary James also Known as M. E. Kerr." Excerpt from *Frankenlouse,* accompanied by information on M. E. Kerr (Fall 1984).

Scholastic *Voice*. "Spotlight on M. E. Kerr and *Little Little*." Interview reprinted in Scholastic Catalogue, 1982.

Stanek, Lou Willett. "A Teacher's Resource to M. E. Kerr." New York: HarperCollins, 1991.

Sutton, Roger. "A Conversation with M. E. Kerr." *School Library Journal* (June 1993): 24–29.

Sweeney, Patricia Runk. "Self-Discovery and Re-Discovery in the Novels of M. E. Kerr." *The Lion and the Unicorn* (Fall 1978): 37–43.

Tallmer, Jerry. "An Old Question for Young Adults." *New York Post* (8 July 1978).

Unsworth, Robert. "Holden Caulfield, Where are You?" *School Library Journal* (January 1977): 40–41.

Zinck, Catherine. "A Record of Epiphanies in the Work of M. E. Kerr." *Virginia English Bulletin* (Winter 1986).

Selected Book Reviews

DELIVER US FROM EVIE

Bushman, Kay Parks. *The ALAN Review* (Fall 1995): unpaged.

Donelson, Kenneth L., and Alleen Pace Nilsen. *English Journal* (November 1995): 97.

Morrow, Claudia. *School Library Journal* (November 1994): 121.

DINKY HOCKER SHOOTS SMACK!

Buckley, Tom. "TV: Afterschool Gluttony." *New York Times* (November 15, 1978): C-30.

Carlson, Dale. "Smack." *New York Times Book Review*, Part 1 (February 11, 1973): 8.

Horn Book (February 1973): 56.

New York Times Book Review (February 11, 1973): 8.

Pollack, Pamela D. *School Library Journal* (December 1972): 67.

Rosenberg, Howard. "Dinky Hocker on ABC." *Los Angeles Times* (November 15, 1978): IV:28.

FELL

Keck, Judith. *The ALAN Review* (Winter 1988): unpaged.

Locke, Susan L. *School Library Journal* (August 1987): 96.

Sutton, Roger. *Bulletin of the Center for Children's Books* 40 (July/August 1987): 212.

Tyson, Christy. *Voice of Youth Advocates* (October 1987): 202.

FELL BACK

Lewis, Marjorie. *School Library Journal* (September 1989): 272.

Rochman, Hazel. *Booklist* 86 (September 15, 1989): 163

Zeiger, Hanna B. *The Horn Book Guide* 1:1 (July-December 1989): 87

FELL DOWN

English Journal (April 1992): 83.

McCutcheon, Laura. *School Library Journal* (October 1991): 145–46.

Rochman, Hazel. *Booklist* 88 (September 15, 1991): 135.

FRANKENLOUSE

Dollisch, Patricia A. *School Library Journal* (November 1994): 104

GENTLEHANDS

Bradford, Richard. "The Nazi Legacy: Undoing History." *New York Times Book Review* (30 April 1978): 30.

Charnes, Ruth. *Interracial Books for Children Bulletin* 9:8 (1978): 18.

Flowers, Ann A. *Horn Book* (June 1978): 284–85.
Pollack, Pamela D. *School Library Journal* (March 1978): 138.
Sutherland, Zena. *Chicago Tribune Book Review* (2 July 1978).

HIM SHE LOVES?
Farmer, Sharron. *Voice of Youth Advocates* (August 1984): 144.
Flowers, Ann A. *Horn Book* (June 1984): 339.
Publishers Weekly (February 24, 1984): 140.

I STAY NEAR YOU
Bulletin of the Center for Children's Books (June 1985): 188.
Larson, Gerry. *School Library Journal* (April 1985): 98.
Tyson, Christy. *Voice of Youth Advocates* (June 1985): 132.

IF I LOVE YOU, AM I TRAPPED FOREVER?
Balducci, Carolyn. *New York Times Book Review* (16 September 1973): 8.
Gersoni-Stavn, Diane. *School Library Journal* (April 1973): 75.
Horn Book (June 1973): 276–77.
Kirkus Reviews (February 1, 1973): 123–24.

I'LL LOVE YOU WHEN YOU'RE MORE LIKE ME
Gerhardt, Lillian N. *School Library Journal* (October 1977): 124–25.
Horn Book (December 1977): 668–69.
Interracial Books for Children Bulletin #3 (1978): 14.
New York Times Book Review (November 13, 1977): 50

IS THAT YOU, MISS BLUE?
Burns, Mary M. *Horn Book* (August 1975): 365.
Gray, Mrs. John G. "Young People's Books." *Best Sellers* (May 1975): 49.
Nelson, Alix. *New York Times Book Review* (April 13, 1975): 8.

LINGER
Codell, Cindy Darling. *School Library Journal* (July 1993): 101
English Journal (January 1994): 79.

LITTLE LITTLE
Abrahamson, Dick. *English Journal* (September 1981): 77.
Heins, Ethel L. *Horn Book* (June 1981): 309.
Kaye, Marilyn. *New York Times Book Review* (May 19, 1981): 38.

LOVE IS A MISSING PERSON
Gerhardt, Lillian N. *School Library Journal* (November 1975): 176.
Publishers Weekly (June 30, 1975): 58.
Sutherland, Zena. *Bulletin of the Center for Children's Books* (November 1975): 48.

ME ME ME ME ME:; NOT A NOVEL
Hammond, Nancy. *Horn Book* (December 1983): 462.
Lewis, Marjorie. *School Library Journal* (August 1983): 77–78.
Milton, Joyce. *New York Times Book Review* (May 11, 1983): 39.

Reed. Arthea. *The ALAN Review* 11:1 (Fall 1983): 29.

NIGHT KITES

Burket, Mary Lou. "Teen-Agers and Troubled Times," *Book World—The Washington Post* (May 11, 1986): 17, 22.

Eaglen, Audrey B. *New York Times Book Review* (April 12, 1986): 30.

Silvey, Anita. *Horn Book* (September-October 1986): 597.

SHOEBAG (UNDER MARY JAMES, PSEUD.)

Ann A. Flowers. *The Horn Book Guide* 1:2 (January-June 1990): 255.

Manning, Patricia. *School Library Journal* (June 1990): 124.

THE SHUTEYES (UNDER MARY JAMES, PSEUD.)

Vose, Ruth. *School Library Journal* (April 1993): 120.

THE SON OF SOMEONE FAMOUS

Best Sellers (April 15, 1974): 54.

Burns, Mary. *Horn Book* (August 1974): 384–85.

Sutherland, Zena. *Bulletin of the Center for Children's Books* (May 1974): 146.

WHAT I REALLY THINK OF YOU?

Digilio, Alice. *Book World—The Washington Post* (July 11, 1982): 11.

Kaye, Marilyn. *New York Times Book Review* (September 12, 1982): 49–50.

Shapiro, L. L. *School Library Journal* (May 1982): 71–72.

Index

The Author

Alleen Pace Nilsen is professor of English at Arizona State University. With Kenneth L. Donelson, she is coauthor of *Literature for Today's Young Adults* (fifth edition, 1997, HarperCollins/Longman), the major United States textbook used to prepare high school teachers and librarians to assist and encourage young people in their independent reading. She is a founding member of the International Society for Humor Studies and writes a "Humor in the News" column for *Humor: International Journal of Humor Research*. She was founding coeditor of *The ALAN Review*, the publication of the Assembly on Literature for Adolescents of the National Council of Teachers of English (NCTE). In 1987 she received the ALAN Award for her contributions to the field of literature for young readers. In 1990 she was the recipient of NCTE's Rewey Belle Inglis Award given annually to an outstanding woman in English education. Her articles on young adult literature regularly appear in the *English Journal* and in *School Library Journal*.

The Editor

Patricia J. Campbell is an author and critic specializing in books for young adults. She has taught adolescent literature at UCLA and is the former Assistant Coordinator of Young Adult Services for the Los Angeles Public Library. Her literary criticism has been published in the *New York Times Book Review* and many other journals. From 1978 to 1988 her column "The YA Perplex," a monthly review of young adult books, appeared in the *Wilson Library Bulletin*. She now writes a column on controversial issues in adolescent literature for *Horn Book* magazine. Campbell is the author of five books, among them *Presenting Robert Cormier,* the first volume in the Twayne Young Adult Author Series. In 1989 she was the recipient of the American Library Association Grolier Award for distinguished achievement with young people and books. A native of Los Angeles, Campbell now lives on an avocado ranch near San Diego, where she and her husband, David Shore, write and publish books on overseas motorhome travel and she heads a literary agency specializing in young adult fiction.